ESTRANGEMENT

Contributions in Philosophy

ESTRANGEMENT

Marx's Conception of Human Nature and the Division of Labor

ISIDOR WALLIMANN

Foreword by Gunter W. Remmling

CONTRIBUTIONS IN PHILOSOPHY, NUMBER 16

Greenwood Press
Westport, Connecticut • London, England

Library of Congress Cataloging in Publication Data

Wallimann, Isidor, 1944–
 Estrangement: Marx's conception of human nature
and the division of labor.

 (Contributions in philosophy; no. 16 ISSN 0084–926X)
 Bibliography: p.
 Includes index.
 1.   Marx, Karl, 1818–1883.   2.   Man.   3.   Division
of labor.   4.   Alienation (Philosophy)   I.   Title.
B3305.M74W34   335.4'12   80–929
ISBN 0-313-22096-4 (lib. bdg.)
Copyright © 1981 by Isidor Wallimann

Library of Congress Catalog Card Number: 80–929
ISBN: 0-313-22096-4
ISSN: 0084–926X
First published in 1981
Greenwood Press
A division of Congressional Information Service, Inc.
88 Post Road West, Westport, Connecticut 06881

Printed in the United States of America

10 9 8 7 6 5 4 3 2 1

Copyright Acknowledgments

The publishers listed below kindly gave me permission to reprint from the following
sources:
 Grundrisse: Foundations of the Critique of Political Economy, by Karl Marx,
translated by Martin Nicolaus. New York: Random House, Inc., 1973. Translation
and Foreword Copyright © 1973 by Martin Nicolaus. Notes Copyright © 1973 by
Ben Fowkes.
 The Ethnological Notebooks, by Karl Marx, transcribed and edited with an in-
troduction by Lawrence Krader. Assen: Van Gorcum & Co., 1974, © 1974 by
Lawrence Krader.
 Collected Works, Vols. 3, 4, 5, 6, by Karl Marx and Friedrich Engels. New York:
International Publishers Co., Inc., 1975-1976. Reprinted by permission of Interna-
tional Publishers Co., Inc., Copyright © 1976.
 Critique of the Gotha Programme, by Karl Marx. New York: International
Publishers Co., Inc., 1938. Copyright 1938 by International Publishers Co., Inc.
 *The Origin of the Family, Private Property and the State: In the Light of the
Researches of Lewis H. Morgan*, by Frederick Engels. New York: International
Publishers Co., Inc., 1942. Copyright 1942 by International Publishers Co., Inc.
 Alienation: From Marx to Modern Sociology, by Joachim Israel. Copyright ©
1971 by Allyn and Bacon, Inc., Boston. Reprinted with permission.

To my mother and
in memory of my father

CONTENTS

FOREWORD BY GUNTER W. REMMLING

When Marx informed his collaborator Arnold Ruge that he had decided to "make man into man," he rejected the notion of a human being as no more than an estranged producer of commodities belonging to someone else. More importantly, Marx had communicated to Ruge the central idea that was to give purpose to his entire life's work: the realization of the true character of men and women. Marx crystallized this idea in the intellectual fires that produced his differentiation from Hegel and Feuerbach. The idea persuaded him to concentrate all his remarkable energies on identifying the forces that could dissolve the contradiction between idea and reality. Therefore, Marx set out to discover those elements in social action that had the power to break down the existing socioeconomic relations—elements that, because of their own inner contradiction, would negate the general estrangement in social life.

Marx understood that these elements had to be found in the relations of active life. He realized that they were present in the relations that dominate as a nameless force the relations between persons—that is, in the economic relations wherein all estrangement originates. While commodities relinquish their ultimate qualities in money, men and women relinquish theirs in becoming commodities; they become commodities as soon as their labor power becomes useless, unless it is sold. In society, the worker is not a human being but merely the exponent of an abstract commodity: labor power. In selling this commodity, the worker sells himself or herself, and thus the estrangement of men and women reaches its ultimate form. The economic theorists of capitalism therefore regard proletarians— the men and women who, without capital or ground rent, live entirely by their labor—as mere workers but not as human beings.

Unlike bourgeois economists and sociologists, Marx viewed the division of labor as problematic. He maintained that the division of labor established the mutual dependence of individuals and introduced the contradiction between the interests of the individual and the common interest of all individuals. In its complete form, the division of labor creates a situation whereby no one any longer disposes over the means of his subsistence. Now the relations of production and trade completely replace human relations, and men and women no longer face each other as men and women but as mere exponents of the anonymous and all-powerful relations of production that separate and estrange one human being from the other. Hence, the discovery of the laws of political economy was at the same time the discovery of the conditions that had to be met in order to achieve the self-realization of the human being. This is the reason for Marx's tireless analysis of economic laws and their development as reflected in his *Kapital* and kindred writings.

Isidor Wallimann's study of Marx's theory of estrangement introduces the long-needed proof that the concept of estrangement remained fundamental to Marx's thought throughout his life's work. Equally important is the author's interpretation of the *involuntary* nature of the division of labor as the fundamental cause of estrangement. Most importantly, Wallimann's work shows in detail that Marx employs two different conceptions of human nature, and it explains how the relative (historical) and nonrelative (biological) conceptions of human nature bear upon Marx's theory of estrangement. For the first time, Wallimann shows that Marx speaks of estrangement only in those instances wherein individuals are prevented from living according to their human nature (biologically conceived). The structure of society prevents individuals from fully exercising the faculties nature has given them: they are estranged. For instance, they are prevented from subjecting their labor power and the product of their labor to their own will, although by nature they are capable of doing so.

Wallimann's interpretation is methodical, rigorous, impeccably judicious, and based on an impressive mastery of the primary and secondary sources. As such, it has raised the standards for academic Marxist scholarship.

Málaga, Spain
November 1979   GUNTER W. REMMLING

PREFACE

While this study owes much to many people in one way or another, here it is possible to express my appreciation only to those who were most directly involved.

Gunter Remmling gave generously of his time and valuable advice. I gained immeasurably from the breadth of his knowledge relating to the work of Karl Marx and other subjects, as well as from the many hours spent in pleasant conversation and friendship. I am also very appreciative of David Edelstein, both for his interest in me and my work, and for his personal encouragement. I am particularly grateful for the many meaningful questions he raised in connection with this study. I would also like to thank him, as well as Ephraim H. Mizruchi and Willie Lamouse-Smith, for their pertinent suggestions. In addition, I am thankful for the academic support and friendship I received from Jerry Jacobs, Harold Orbach, George Zito, Nicholas Tatsis, Barry Glassner, Allen Large, and Dorothy Zito.

This study also owes much to Linda Brasington who devoted much effort and patience to the typing of a manuscript interspersed with so many awkward foreign and English words; and to my friend, Carol Leonard, without whose emotional support and direct involvement in the editions of the material, this study would not have been possible. A research grant from Syracuse University and support from Hobart and William Smith Colleges facilitated this study considerably.

Finally, I would like to extend my gratitude to the staff of Greenwood Press for devoting many hours of careful work to this manuscript and giving useful advice on numerous occasions. I would especially like to thank James Sabin, Margaret Brezicki, Kathie Stone, and Anne Kugielsky.

INTRODUCTION

Although the term "alienation" is used frequently in popular and scientific circles, its precise meaning remains so unclear that many have questioned its value. Because the term has been imprecisely used and because present-day usage seems equally imprecise, it has also been recommended that the term "alienation" be either abandoned or conceptually clarified and more rigorously defined.

This study attempts to show that Marx used the terms "alienation" and "estrangement" both precisely and systematically, and that calls for the abandonment or clarification of the terms are unjustified with regard to the works of Marx. We are not convinced, however, that the lack of precision inherent in today's use of the term "alienation" is reversible and that the term is at all useful as it has been employed in modern studies. It is therefore important to distinguish strictly between Marx's precision and today's ambiguity and thus to abandon the widely held notion that many modern studies involving the term are somehow related to the Marxian tradition, when in fact they are not.

There are several reasons for today's lack of consensus and systematic use of the term "alienation." In this short space, we can only briefly touch upon some of them. As used in popular language today, the term designates individual or group remoteness from and/or disaffection with something or someone. It may therefore be said that "alienation" stands for a discrepancy of some sort. Contemporary social scientists—not immune from the influence of popular language—design studies intending to locate and measure the individual's "alienation." Thus, for example, the individual's alienation (that is, remoteness or disaffection) from government or the political process is studied, and phrases such as "urban alienations" (Fischer, 1973) are coined.

In view of the multitude of cases in which it is possible to speak of remoteness or disaffection, "alienation" loses all specificity. It is at best a sophisticated term denoting a variety of conditions that could, without loss of clarity, be just as well apprehended with numerous other words. In fact, the use of vocabulary other than "alienation" to describe situations in which individuals or groups are remote from someone or something and/or are disaffected about something would most likely lead to increased specificity in the way language is used to describe social phenomena, by both laymen and social scientists. Instead of an all-encompassing term such as "alienation," terms more descriptive of various types of remoteness and disaffection could be employed. Certainly, this would not be a violation of the spirit of the "social science enterprise." On the contrary, social science as well as philosophy depends on a disciplined use of vocabulary in its attempt to apprehend reality.

Given the all-encompassing way in which "alienation" is often used, it is indeed understandable why some advocate dropping the term altogether from the social science vocabulary. Indeed, it does not seem to be necessary for a clear understanding of the various types of remoteness or disaffection. In actuality, the particularity of these various types, which are of special interest to social scientists *because of their particularity*, tends to be glossed over when "alienation" is used.

Of course, "alienation" is not always employed in an all-encompassing and indiscriminate way. Thus, attempts have been made to arrive at particular dimensions that could be subsumed under the term—that is, to apprehend particular situations of individuals' remoteness or disaffection. Seeman's six varieties of alienation (1976:268) serve as an example. These varieties (powerlessness, meaninglessness, normlessness, cultural estrangement, self-estrangement, and social isolation) represent an effort to avoid using a term that is too all-encompassing. It remains unclear, however, why the term "alienation," when used in this way, should be retained at all. There is no apparent advantage, for example, in calling "social isolation" a variety of alienation. "Social isolation," however defined, remains social isolation.

It also remains unclear why only some situations and not others are categorized as "varieties of alienation." The criteria for categorization have been quite arbitrary ones and are likely to remain so. For example, Seeman's "varieties of alienation" only reflect one person's judgment and attempt to abstract from the numerous ways in which the term "alienation" is used. It represents an attempt to create a consensus concerning the use of the term where there is no consensus. The basis on which this consensus could rest is in itself relative, making it both unlikely that a discipline-wide consensus could be sustained and that "alienation" as a term would be given a clearly defined meaning in the social science community.

Seeman's endeavor, then, does represent an attempt to clearly define and consistently apply the term "alienation." But the attempt has not been successful and the ambiguity often associated with today's use of the term has hardly been overcome. Recent social analysis has often linked the use of the term to Marx and has justified it on the basis of his writings. In many cases, however, this linking has explicitly or implicitly distorted Marx's thought and the way he used the terms "alienation" and "estrangement."

The present study addresses the main distortions that have arisen from linking Marx to modern research and commentary on "alienation." It also attempts to break some new ground in interpreting Marx and points out the implications for scholars who wish to utilize Marx's concepts of estrangement and alienation[1] in their own work. The aim here is both to contribute to the understanding of Marx's work and to promote greater clarity and rigor in the way certain concepts, especially "estrangement" and "alienation," are used in the social sciences.

In addition to making certain that the correct vocabulary and translations are used when discussing Marx's theory of estrangement, it is equally important that Marx's analytic framework as a whole be understood correctly. Only then is it possible to apprehend the function and value of his theory of estrangement for today's social sciences. Marx based his theory of estrangement on an "inventory" of each human being's capabilities. In his investigation of the nature of social organization, he found that throughout most of history individuals have not been able to live according to their capabilities. For example, by nature human beings are capable of subjecting production and the product of their labor to their conscious control. Yet, in actual life they are prevented from doing so. In other words, a discrepancy was found to exist between individuals' capabilities and how, in fact, they must live. Individuals were seen to be estranged in the broadest sense of the word. More concretely, taking capitalism as an example, Marx showed *why* a discrepancy existed between individuals' capabilities and how in fact they must live. He specified precisely the social processes that force individuals into such a discrepancy. He also specified the basis upon which it can be said that individuals are estranged and from what they are estranged.

For Marx, the desired form of social organization was communism, which, contrary to capitalism, would assure that individuals would be able to live according to their capabilities. Thus, the need for a communist society as perceived by Marx was based on the value judgment that individuals should be able to live according to their capabilities. Marx's call for a communist society did not, of course, only express the wish that individuals be able to live according to their capabilities. Marx maintained that once human beings have the opportunity to live according to their abilities, many other conditions would change for the better. Therefore, man would no longer be dominated by the product of his own labor, and his physical existence would no longer be subject to arbitrary exchange relations. Hence, the call for a society without estrangement is not based only on the abstract postulate that man ought to be able to live according to his capabilities. Marx also realized that if estrangement were not eliminated, the undesirable conditions of life brought about by capitalist social organization could not be abolished.

According to Marx, a form of social organization such as that which is prevalent under capitalism develops its own forces which in various ways will set the stage for the successful construction of a communist society. Marx did not advocate a society without estrangement only because of an abstract notion that it is desirable that individuals be able to live according to their nature. Rather, he asserted that if and only if individuals are able to live according to their abilities, which they possess by nature, will it be possible to free humanity of the numerous burdens brought about by a form of social organization (for example, capitalism) which does not allow man to live according to his nature. For Marx, the ability to live according to one's abilities was not completely subject to the will of individuals. Sufficient historical development was seen as a necessary prerequisite to the successful formation of a society in which individuals would be able to live according to their nature.

This study shows that Marx considers estrangement to be a dichotomous phenomenon. If, as is the case under capitalism, individuals are prevented from living according to their capabilities, they are estranged. Evidence is presented here showing that individuals cannot be said to be more or less estranged[2] if Marx is not to be misinterpreted. For Marx individuals are either estranged or not estranged.

Marx's theory of estrangement becomes a tool for the critical analysis of the capitalist as well as socialist societies known to us today. It is a tool for the critical analysis of all forms of social organization in which individuals are prevented from living according to their abilities.

NOTES

1. As the title of this study indicates, I do not speak of Marx's theory of *alienation* but of his theory of *estrangement*. Marx made a clear distinction between the terms "estrangement" (*Entfremdung*) and "alienation" (*Entäusserung*), and the two terms should not both be translated as "alienation," as customarily has been the case. Based on inadequate translations, social scientists in the English-speaking world have seldom made this distinction, which is so crucial to an understanding of Marx.

2. In this context, it will also become apparent that many studies involving Marx's theory of estrangement have overlooked this important fact.

ABBREVIATIONS

German Sources[1] *Volume No.*	*English Sources*[2] *Volume No.*	*Title*
MEW, EB, 1.T.	CW, 3	*Economic and Philosophic Manuscripts of 1844*
MEW, 2	CW, 4	*The Holy Family*
MEW, 3	CW, 5	*Theses on Feuerbach*
MEW, 3	CW, 5	*The German Ideology*
MEW, 4	CW, 6	*The Poverty of Philosophy*
MEW, 4	CW, 6	*Manifesto of the Communist Party*
MEW, G	G	*Grundrisse*
MEW, 13	CPE	*A Contribution to the Critique of Political Economy*
MEW, 16	WPP	*Wages, Price and Profit*
MEW, 19	CGP	*Critique of the Gotha Programme*

1. Marx/Engels: *Werke* (MEW).
2. Marx/Engels: *Collected Works* (CW).

MEW, 20	AD	*Herr Eugen Dühring's Revolution in Science (Anti-Dühring)*
MEW, 21	OF	*The Origin of the Family, Private Property, and the State*
MEW, 23	C1	*Capital* Vol. I
MEW, 24	C2	*Capital* Vol. II
MEW, 25	C3	*Capital* Vol. III
MEW, 26.1	TS1	*Theories of Surplus-Value* I
MEW, 26.2	TS2	*Theories of Surplus-Value* II
MEW, 26.3	TS3	*Theories of Surplus-Value* III
	EN	*The Ethnological Notebooks of Karl Marx*

ESTRANGEMENT

1

ISSUES AND PROCEDURES

In the 1920s, along with the ascent of the Frankfurt School, Marxian thought experienced a revival that had far-reaching effects. The revival occurred in a political atmosphere that, to say the least, was quite pluralistic. The Weimar Republic, despite its short life-span (1919-1933), presented a stage on which, as Remmling (1973:3-43) has pointed out, marginal characters in the society could suddenly become socially accepted major characters (see also Meja, 1975). Thus, very unlike the situation during Weber's imperial Germany, Marxists were suddenly found at the university. This increasingly "tolerant" environment also provided fertile ground for thinkers like Mannheim who drew heavily from Marx and whose intellectual questions pertaining to the sociology of knowledge might easily be viewed as socially threatening (Remmling, 1975).

Given the revival of Marxism and the interest in the sociology of knowledge in Weimar Germany, it is therefore not surprising that renewed attention was also paid to Marx's theory of estrangement. In fact, this theory must be considered a central element in the evaluation of his contribution to the sociology of knowledge (Remmling, 1967). Outside the particular sphere of the sociology of knowledge, Marcuse (1964, 1970, 1972) and Fromm (1961, 1968)—

both members of the Frankfurt School—made extensive use of Marx's concept of estrangement in their writings.

Given this initial momentum, many social scientists became interested in further employing Marx's theory of estrangement in their social analyses. In retrospect, it has become apparent that many questions concerning the applicability and interpretation of Marx's theory have not been resolved. If there is to be a common discourse, and if Marx's theory of estrangement is to be employed fruitfully, it is essential that sociologists share a common understanding of the nature of this theory. This study addresses itself to some of these still unresolved questions and represents an attempt both to give a logically consistent interpretation of Marx's theory of estrangement and to point out the scope of its applicability. In short, the questions addressed here can be stated in the following way.

—What is Marx's concept of human nature?
—Is there only one theory of estrangement in Marx?
—Is estrangement measurable: Does what Marx calls estrangement cause certain behavior, feelings, or attitudes?
—Is Marx's theory of estrangement also applicable to noncapitalist societies?
—Is estrangement as Marx views it a historically specific phenomenon, or is it an existential predicament?
—What role does the division of labor play in Marx's theory of estrangement?

Unfortunately, students of Marx writing in the English language (and many in French) have generally not made a distinction between "estrangement" and "alienation." One of the latest examples of this tendency can be found in Ollman (1976:47, 132), in which "estrangement" and "alienation" are synonyms. Unlike the work done by the Italian scholars (see Bedeschi, 1968, and Chiodi, 1976) who are more precise, both the translations and the use of *Entfremdung* and *Entäusserung* in the English-speaking world are inexact. As one translator points out:

There can hardly be said to be any very common practice among English translators. Thus, M. Milligan (*Economic and Philosophical MSS of 1844*; cit.) translates *Entfremdung* as "estrangement" and *Entäusserung* as "alienation" (or "externalisation"); T. Bottomore (*Karl Marx: Early Writings*) claims that Marx does not distinguish between the two terms and translates both as "alienation" (or "estrangement"). D. McLellan (*Karl Marx: Early Texts*) and L. D. Easton and K. H. Guddat (*Writings of the Young Marx*) translate *Entfremdung* as "alienation" and *Entäusserung* as "externalisation" (Chiodi, 1976:124).

As will become clear in the course of this study, Marx does make a distinction between *Entfremdung* and *Entäusserung*. This distinction, though fine, is an important one and will be discussed later in this work. One qualification is necessary here. The distinction is not, of course, injected into those primary and secondary sources quoted which lack such a distinction, in order to preserve the authenticity of the sources. Hence, in all quotes, except those from the *Collected Works*, the reader should know that whenever the word "alienation" appears, it may actually mean "estrangement."

Social scientists and philosophers generally agree that if someone is said to be estranged, he/she must be estranged *from* something or somebody. What is less often understood is the basis upon which Marx can say that someone is estranged, that is, the element distinguishing Marx's theory of estrangement from, say, a purely nominalist use of the concept of estrangement, according to which individuals are arbitrarily said to be estranged from all sorts of things. On the basis of his concept of human nature, Marx can say that individuals are estranged. Because Marx uses his concept of human nature as a basis for determining why man is estranged, he avoids making only tautological statements[1] and having to give reasons of only a relativistic nature. Thus, Marx's theory of estrangement rests on a concept of human nature that allows for statements about man's estrangement, statements that are neither tautological nor relativistic.[2] This concept can be termed "human nature in general." Generally, the literature dealing with Marx's theory of estrangement (or with his concept of human nature) either fails to make this crucial distinction or fails to make it clearly (for example, Marković, 1974:217-218). The present study shows that such a distinction can be made, and even *must* be made, if Marx's theory of estrangement is to be properly understood and interpreted.

Marx's theory of estrangement cannot be understood without an understanding of *why* man is estranged. When discussing this theory, students of Marx usually focus on wage labor and the accompanying production of commodities. Estrangement is usually, and correctly, said to result from the fact that man must sell his labor power and that he controls neither the product of his labor nor the act of production. However, Marx also speaks of the propertied class as being estranged, even though this class need not sell its labor power. The selling of one's labor power is therefore not the sole explanation for man's estrangement. As this study demonstrates, for Marx the existence of an involuntary division of labor ultimately determines why man is estranged. Conversely, the voluntary division of labor under communism creates a condition of nonestrangement. Thus far, scholars have pointed out only that there is a connection between Marx's theory of estrangement and what he considered to be an involuntary division of labor (Remmling, 1967:152; Mészáros, 1972:140-143). This present investigation, however, shows in more detail not only that the "division of labor" is of central importance in Marx's theory of estrangement, but also how it must be understood. In the process, it will become obvious that for Marx "division of labor" has a much broader meaning than most writers on estrangement have assigned to it. In Marx, division of labor is not exclusively identified with the tendency to divide work into more and more minute tasks. Neither can it be identified only with what some might call the "man as cog in a wheel phenomenon." The discussion in this work of the importance the division of labor plays in Marx's theory of estrangement will also enable the reader to systematically deal with the question as to whether or not, according to Marx, one can speak of estrangement under feudalism[3] and present-day socialism, a topic also addressed by Ota Šik (1972) and Schwarz (1967:82). Schwarz maintains that once the private ownership in the means of production is abolished, it is no longer possible to speak of estrangement, while Šik tends to take the opposite point of view.

This analysis will also show that Marx does not require the abolition of *all* division of labor if man is to live free from estrangement. Marx's aim is not so much to do away with all division of labor as to create a society that allows individuals to engage in a division of labor voluntarily. This is not to say that a voluntary division of labor would not be different along various dimensions from an involuntary one. Rather, individuals are not estranged, even if they should engage in a certain division of labor, as long as they can do so voluntarily.

Any study dealing with the interpretation and application of Marx's theory of estrangement must address the question as to whether it is legitimate to speak of only *one* theory of estrangement. This topic has been under discussion for a considerable length of time, whereby some (such as Mészáros, 1972; Petrović, 1967; E. Fischer, 1970) represent the point of view that there is no difference between Marx's early and later writings. Others maintain that Marx abandoned his theory of estrangement in favor of a theory of reification in his later writings (Israel, 1971). (For a similar argument, see also Swingewood, 1975: 95-97.) Bell (1967:365) states that "the historical Marx had, in effect, repudiated the idea of alienation," a proposition that Mészáros (1972) vigorously counters. Based on the view that the division of labor plays a central role in Marx's theory of estrangement, it will be shown how the issues raised by this rather fruitless debate can be "resolved" and in what sense it is possible to speak of only one theory of estrangement in Marx.

In his excellent review essay on estrangement, Ludz (1973:27) mentions that, in the contemporary use of Marx's theory of estrangement, different "ideological realms as well as divergent methodologies confront one another." Ludz correctly states that some authors believe that "[f]rom Marxist and neo-Marxist points of view, alienation in the hands of empirical-analytical researchers has become merely 'a concept of accommodation' rather than a means of cultural criticism." It is legitimate to ask for the basis of this belief. One source of contention lies in the fact that in contemporary usage of Marx's theory of estrangement, the attempt is made to operationalize "estrangement" in order to make it "accessible" to measurement. The operationalization has frequently been based on social-psychological concepts, implying that if individuals did not perceive their existence and social environment in certain ways, they would not be estranged. Estrangement thus came to be viewed as a function of the individual's state of mind. Others contended that for Marx estrangement was at least in part, if not totally, also a function of certain social-structural conditions (see Schacht, 1971:172; and Israel, 1971). According to this latter view, it follows that if estrangement is to be abolished, basic social-structural changes must occur. This demand for social change is not necessarily implied in the position which holds that estrangement is only a function of whether individuals perceive their social environment in a particular way. In view of this debate, this study investigates whether, according to Marx, estrangement must be viewed as a function of social structure or as one of the individual's states of mind.

Contemporary application of Marx's theory of estrangement raises other crucial issues. Thus, many students of Marx who interpret and apply his theory of estrangement view estrangement as occurring to a greater or lesser extent.[4] It is also very common to view estrangement as a cause for certain behavior, feelings, or attitudes. Both of these views are discussed in detail, and it will become apparent how the application of Marx's theory of estrangement is intricately linked with its interpretation. It will also become apparent that *any* attempt to measure estrangement, that is, to view it in quantitative terms, is problematic. The problem with measurement, as will be shown, does not lie with the multidimensionality of estrangement as Feuer (1963:139-140) seems to think,[5] but with the implicit danger of misinterpreting Marx once estrangement is perceived to be a quantitative phenomenon.

The early postwar period witnessed an upsurge and popularization of existentialist thinking which did not leave the debate on estrangement unaffected. The years in which existentialism experienced its growth were . also characterized by an increased interest in Marx's early writings, particularly the *Manuscripts.* For many, the *Manuscripts* were symbolic of the "revitalization" of Marxism and a "novel" source for an attempt to provide new interpretations of and insights into Marx in view of the Stalinist experience. Marxist scholarship had become a "weapon" that could be directed against both capitalism and "Russian socialism." Thus, it is not surprising that philosophers from socialist countries were put on alert. What produced a virtual counteroffensive, however, was the fact that existentialists like Sartre made heavy use of the concept of estrangement in their writings. Scholars like Schaff (1964), Oiserman (1965), and Schwarz (1967) subsequently accused Sartre and others of misinterpreting Marx. They claimed that the existentialists treated estrangement as if it were a phenomenon of all social life at all times, and they maintained that Marx thought estrangement should be associated with only a certain historical phase.[6] As a result of the investigation in this volume (including the topics of scarcity and estrangement in present-day socialism), it will become clear how the issues raised above must be resolved. I do not endorse Jordan's (1971:19) view that "Marx came to believe that estrangement (self-alienation) is an unavoidable consequence of the necessity to work."

Focusing on the issues outlined above may give us the key to a novel interpretation of Marx's theory of estrangement. The contribution this study makes with respect to the interpretation of Marx's writings will be of immediate relevance to the social sciences which have traditionally sought to employ his theory for further social analysis. It will be of immediate relevance to social science in the same way that the social scientists' application of the theory has affected its interpretation.

This inquiry seeks to give an accurate and well-documented interpretation of Marx's theory of estrangement. Hence, I rely on the Marx/Engels *Werke* as the source of Marx's original writings.[7] The translations of the relevant passages are taken from the sources indicated in the list of abbreviations. As a rule, all the translations provided here have been examined for their accuracy.[8] Whenever the translation does not accurately convey the meaning of the original, it is amended. Any such alteration is indicated, and usually the justification for making a specific change is presented.

This text deliberately excludes controversies concerning interpretations of what Marx says on certain topics in order to avoid confusion and overloading the text with too many details. In the process, it is hoped that the main theses of this book will also appear with greater clarity. This does not mean that points of controversy are not discussed. They are indeed addressed, but only in footnotes and in sections separately set aside for this purpose. The various interpretations of Marx are for the most part in those sections labeled "Introduction," "Discussion," "Comment," and the whole of Chapters 1, 9, and 10.

This work differs from similar studies in its conscious attempt to separate the account of Marx's thought from points of debate and in its use of complete quotes. In general, I refrain from quoting "phrases," and use full quotes for purposes of documentation. Seldom is there paraphrasing without subsequent documentation by quotes. There are several reasons why this procedure is followed. First, any interpretative study depends for its "data" on the texts that are being interpreted. It is therefore very important that these data be presented in an unabridged form. An interpretation documented by complete quotes presents less risk of distorting the meaning than does an interpretation based on paraphrase or quotation of phrases. Second, the reader will be directly involved in the ways Marx expresses himself, an emotional component that should not be separated from an attempt to understand Marx. Third, the reader's direct confrontation with Marx's text (as well as the reader's development of a feeling for it) facilitates a critical appraisal of the interpretation in this book, and allows a more objective debate. While this approach does not guarantee a solution to all the questions of interpretation, it is at least a step in the right direction. In order to improve the readability of the "main text," quotes that provide additional evidence for a certain argument are presented in the appropriate notes.

NOTES

1. For example, "man is estranged because he is distant from, or does not control such and such."

2. It also allows for statements that are empirically founded. Mandel (1971:161) is incorrect when he says that early writings lack "empirical foundations" and are "largely philosophical and speculative." Mandel's misunderstanding comes from the fact that he does not fully appreciate the role Marx's concept of human nature plays with respect to his theory of estrangement.

3. Feudalism is characterized by the almost total absence of a market in labor power. Ollman (1976: 181, 252) points out that Marx speaks of estrangement under feudalism, but he does not elaborate on the subject.

4. See, for example, Swingewood (1975:92) and Krader (1975a:269; 1975b:437).

5. The problem, then, is not how to measure a phenomenon which some (Neal and Rettig, 1967; Tatsis and Zito, 1975) claim is multidimensional. Rather, the problem is whether what Marx called estrangement is at all accessible to measurement, if Marx is not to be misinterpreted.

6. Similarly, others can be criticized: "The glaring survival of phenomena of alienation in Soviet society serves as a basis for bourgeois ideologists to demonstrate triumphantly the absolute inevitability of alienation 'in industrial society' " (Mandel, 1971:187).

7. An exception is *The Poverty of Philosophy* which was translated into German under Engels' supervision (see MEW, 4, pp. 558-569, 621).

8. This does not imply that the translations are optimal with respect to clarity and style. To provide optimal translations was beyond the province of this work.

2

Marx's Conception of Human Nature

Marx's theory of estrangement is rooted directly in his theory of human nature. Before addressing the issue of what leads to estrangement, I will therefore examine the ways in which Marx's theory depends on his definition of human nature.

When defining the characteristics that make man specifically human, Marx makes use of two different starting points which yield quite different definitions of human nature. First, he defines human nature using a biological model, and then an historical model. In the course of the discussion here, it will become evident that Marx's theory of estrangement is based primarily on the biological model. This is not to say that Marx was not interested in the historical, for he used the historical model to counter the views of some of his most ardent intellectual competitors, as is evident when one reads, for example, *The German Ideology*.

MAN VERSUS ANIMAL: THE BIOLOGICAL MODEL

The biological model of human nature is a continuous theme in Marx, appearing in both his early and later works. The same is true with regard to Marx's historical model. He states that what is unique to the human species from a biological point of view are the very general ways in which human beings differ from animals. As is indicated by the currently used definition *homo sapiens* (a term Marx does not tend to use but to which he would probably have no objections), human beings are knowing beings with a consciousness and the ability to reflect upon themselves and their human and natural environment. As a result, unlike the animals, human beings have a sense of history and can anticipate the future. They can consciously and willfully create and produce for a manifold of purposes, as individuals and as a collective. Marx does not claim that his method (that is, isolating what is specifically human by contrasting human beings with animals) is new. On the contrary, he maintains that, since Aristotle and the Stoics, it has been common knowledge that human beings have "intellect, emotion and will" (CW, 5, p. 511; MEW, 3, p. 500). Marx believes that his premises with regard to the differences between human beings and animals are not arbitrary, but rather are empirically verifiable: "The premises from which we begin are not arbitrary ones, not dogmas, but real premises from which abstraction can only be made in the imagination . . . . These premises can thus be verified in a purely empirical way" (CW, 5, p. 31; MEW, 3, p. 20). With respect to the differences between man and the animals he states:

> The animal is immediately one with its life activity. It does not distinguish itself from it. It is *its life activity*. Man makes his life activity itself the object of his will and of his consciousness. He has conscious life activity. It is not a determination with which he directly merges. Conscious life-activity distinguishes man immediately from animal life (CW, 3, p. 276); MEW, EB 1.T., p. 516).

> Admittedly animals also produce. . . . But an animal only produces what it immediately needs for itself or its young. It produces one-sidedly, whilst man produces universally. It produces only under the dominion of immediate physical need, whilst man produces even when he is free from physical need and only truly produces in freedom therefrom. An animal produces only itself, whilst man reproduces the whole of nature. An animal's product belongs immediately to its physical body, whilst man freely confronts his product. An animal forms objects only in accordance with the standard and the need of the species to which it belongs, whilst man knows how to apply everywhere the inherent standard to the object. Man therefore also forms objects in accordance with the laws of beauty (CW, 3, pp. 276-277; MEW, EB, 1.T., p. 517).

Men can be distinguished from animals by consciousness, by religion or anything else you like. They themselves begin to distinguish themselves from animals as soon as they begin to *produce* their means of subsistence, a step which is conditioned by their physical organisation. By producing their means of subsistence men are indirectly producing their material life (CW, 5, p. 31; MEW, 3, p. 21).

Language, like consciousness, only arises from the need, the necessity, of intercourse with other men. Where there exists a relationship, it exists for me: the animal does not "relate" itself to anything, it does not "relate" itself at all. For the animal its relation to others does not exist as a relation (CW, 5, p. 44; MEW, 3, p. 30).

At this point [i.e., at the beginning of conscious social life] man is distinguished from sheep only by the fact that with him consciousness takes the place of instinct or that his instinct is a conscious one (CW, 5, p. 44; MEW, 3, p. 31).

But what distinguishes the worst architect from the best of bees is this, that the architect raises his structure in imagination before he erects it in reality. At the end of every labour-process, we get a result that already existed in the imagination of the labourer at its commencement. He not only effects a change of form in the material on which he works, but he also realises a purpose of his own that gives the law to his modus operandi, and to which he must subordinate his will. And this subordination is no mere momentary act. Besides the exertion of the bodily organs, the process demands that, during the whole operation, the workman's will be steadily in consonance with his purpose. This means close attention. The less he is attracted by the nature of the work, and the mode in which it is carried on, and the less, therefore, he enjoys it as something which gives play to his bodily and mental powers, the more close his attention is forced to be (C1, p. 174; MEW, 23, p. 193).

In postulating that, contrary to animals, human beings produce independently of need, Marx disagrees with Adam Smith. Adam Smith assumes that human beings by nature, prefer rest (*Ruhe*) to work, while Marx postulates that the individual, by nature, tends also to engage in work.

Nonetheless, Marx would probably agree with the suggestion that under certain historical circumstances, individuals prefer rest to work. In a society in which work is not imposed on individuals (a subject discussed), however, Marx would maintain that this is not the case (MEW, G, pp. 505, 507):

"it seems quite far from Smith's mind that the individual, 'in his normal state of health, strength, activity, skill, facility,' also needs a normal portion of work, and of the suspension of tranquillity" (G, p. 611); MEW, G, p. 505).

If Marx is willing to admit that under given circumstances human beings might prefer rest (*Ruhe*) to work, in order to be consistent, he must also admit that individuals may not behave or be able to behave in a way that corresponds to their "natural condition." This "natural condition" is a nonvariable (disregarding human evolution) condition, since, according to Marx himself, it is based not on dogma but on observable, empirical reality, a collection of facts derived from a comparison of the human being with animals. As a result, one can speak of human nature in *general*—human nature, a "natural condition," which exists uninfluenced by the course of history. Against Jeremy Bentham, Marx argues therefore that general human nature cannot be defined from the utility theory, since what is useful is historically relative and general human nature is in no way relative:

> To know what is useful for a dog, one must study dog-nature. This nature itself is not to be deduced from the principle of utility. Applying this to man, he that would criticise all human acts, movements, relations, etc., by the principle of utility, must first deal with human nature as modified in each historical epoch. Bentham makes short work of it. With the driest naïveté he takes the modern shopkeeper, especially the English shop keeper, as the normal man. Whatever is useful to this queer normal man, and to his world, is absolutely useful (C1, p. 571; MEW, 23, p. 637).

As this quotation indicates, Marx also makes use of an historical model of human nature.

THE BEHAVIOR OF INDIVIDUALS CHANGES:
THE HISTORICAL MODEL

Bentham, using the principle of utility, arrived at a definition of human nature or "normal man" (*Normalmensch*). Marx objects to this definition, arguing that Bentham's "normal man" is a mere historical phenomenon. Therefore, in addition to his theory of general human nature, Marx introduces a theory of specific human nature. Human nature as it is understood, in addition to the criteria that distinguish human beings from animals, is accordingly seen to be a function of history. Thus, what for Bentham is "normal man," that is, human nature as such, is for Marx merely human nature as manifested in Bentham's historical period. With Bentham, as with many other philosophers, especially the German idealists, Marx is quick to point out that what is often seen to constitute immutable human nature is not immutable, but represents human traits under certain historical circumstances only. While Marx's biological model emphasizes the properties of human nature that are immutable (such as intellect, consciousness, will, and emotion), his historical model points to the properties of human nature that are subject to change. Marx illustrates this important distinction as follows:

> But in any case, why should the Germans brag so loudly of their knowledge of human essence, since their knowledge does not go beyond the three general attributes, intellect, emotion and will, which have been fairly universally recognised since the days of Aristotle and the Stoics (CW, 5, pp. 511-512; MEW, 3, p. 500).

He also criticizes Herr Karl Grün for his conception of human nature.

> It is obvious too that this "whole man," "contained" in a single attribute of a real individual and interpreted by the philosopher in terms of that attribute, is a complete chimera. Anyway, what sort of man is this "man" who is not seen in his real historical activity and existence, but can be deduced from the lobe of his own ear, or from some other feature which distinguishes him from the animals?

Similarly, Marx criticizes Feuerbach:

> Feuerbach resolves the essence of religion into the essence of man. But the essence of man is no abstraction inherent in each single individual. In its reality it is the ensemble of the social relations.

> Feuerbach, who does not enter upon a criticism of this real essence, is hence obliged:
> 1) To abstract from the historical process and to define the religious sentiment (*Gemüt*) by itself, and to presuppose an abstract—*isolated*—human individual (CW, 5, pp. 7-8; MEW, 3, p. 6).

We can see that Marx accepts a biological definition of human nature, but, as is clear from his comment on Herr Grün, this definition is not sufficient to understand other aspects of human nature. Thus, he introduces the notion that all the aspects of human nature that cannot be derived from a comparison of human beings with animals can be understood by seeing them in an historical perspective. In the same vein, he criticizes those (Grün, Feuerbach, and others) who attempt to understand the nonbiologically based aspects of human nature in ways other than through historical spectacles. He accuses them of "abstracting" and creating "phantasies" about human nature, of falling into the trap of seeing nonbiologically based aspects as absolute instead of mutable and relative.

HUMAN NATURE AND MARX'S DEFINITION
OF MAN AS SPECIES-BEING

If a significant portion of Marx's definition of human nature rests on the comparison of man with animals, so does his concept of species. "Yet productive life is the life of the species" (CW, 3, p. 276). When specifying the type of productive life which defines the species, Marx says:

> It is life-engendering life. The whole character of a species—its species-character—is contained in the character of its life activity; and free, conscious activity is man's species-character . . . . Conscious life activity distinguishes man immediately from animal life activity. It is just because of this that he is a species-being. Or it is only because he is a species-being that he is a conscious being, i.e., that his own life is an object for him. Only because of that is his activity free activity" (CW, 3, p. 276; MEW, EB 1.T., p. 516).

It can readily be seen that, for Marx, the concept of species has a biological base. It is also clear that, on the basis of consciousness, unlike the animals, man is able to reflect upon himself and recognize what makes him a unique, that is, a species-being, when compared to the rest of his nonhuman environment.

> Man is a species-being, not only because in practice and in theory he adopts the species (his own as well as those of other things) as his object, but—and this is only another way of expressing it—also because he treats himself as a *universal* and therefore a free being (CW, 3, p. 275; MEW, EB 1.T., p. 515).

Since these characteristics, if based on the comparison of man with animals, are an integral part of all human beings, it has been possible to see them also as the characterizing elements of the human species. Thus, "species" is defined by the sum of the parts (that is, individuals) possessing the set of characteristics outlined above. However, this gives an atomistic view of what the human species is and does not show that the parts within this species interact with each other. In the *Manuscripts*, Marx postulates that individuals stand in interaction with each other. It is in the *Grundrisse*, however, that he postulates that human interaction is qualitatively very different from that of animals. He adds that precisely this qualitative difference further characterizes the human species:

> The fact that this need on the part of one can be satisfied by the product of the other, and vice versa, and that the one is capable of producing the object of the other's need, this proves that each of them reaches beyond his own particular need etc., as a *human being*, and that they relate to one another as human beings; that all know their species nature (*Gattungswesen*) to be social (*gemeinschaftlich*). It does not happen elsewhere—that elephants produce for tigers, or animals for other animals. For example. A hive of bees comprises at bottom (*au fond*) only one bee, and they all produce the same thing (MEW, G, pp. 154-155; translation mine).[1]

Marx further illustrates the social nature of man, as follows: "If man is confronted by himself, he is confronted by the other man . . . in fact, every relationship in which man [stands] to himself, is realised and expressed only in the relationship in which a man stands to other men" (MEW, EB 1.T., p. 518; translation mine).[2] The above passages show that man is by nature a social being and that this aspect also characterizes the human species as a species. It also is species-nature. Before leaving this discussion, a few comments on Marx's terminology (such as species and species-being) and on interpretations of Marx are in order.

DISCUSSION

Marx's vocabulary has caused some discomfort among scholars, partially because when translated into English, his terminology is often difficult and his word-combinations awkward. Even in German, Marx's terminology concerning the subject of species is not always completely clear, and close attention must be paid to the various twists associated with a particular usage of words. Hence, a short digression on his use of the term *species* in its various combinations may be useful.

"Species" is a translation of *Gattung*, a word that has the following synonyms in German (Klappenbach and Steinitz, 1971): *Art* (translated by Cassell as kind, species, variety, type, sort; race, class, stock, breed; nature) and *Sorte* (translated by Cassell as kind, sort, type, species, quality, grade, variety, brand). *Gattung* itself is translated by Cassell as kind, class, type, sort; species; genus, race, breed, family (of plants) (Betteridge, 1975). A dictionary used in Marx's time translates *Gattung* as kind, sort, species, race (Adler, 1864). Thus, the term *Gattung* can take on various meanings and can be used and translated very flexibly.

The above cited *Wörterbuch der deutschen Gegenwartssprache* (Klappenbach and Steinitz) gives the following description of *Gattung*: general concept which summarizes individual things or beings that have common essential properties" (translation mine). This is how Marx defined what is human nature and species-nature, namely, by singling out those aspects of man that are not subject to historical change, yet distinguish him from the animals. On the basis of these aspects he called man a *Gattung*.

Gattung is usually translated as "species," a word that is generally used in biology for those types of animals that can reproduce themselves. When Marx speaks of *Gattung*, however, he does not have this meaning in mind. For him, man belongs to a species because of the aspects that separate him from the animals and that he has in common with other human beings, including *the fact that man is social*. "Species-being" therefore means "interactive-being," in addition to a being that has intellect, will, and emotion.

Whenever Marx uses the word "species," he may or may not imply all the characteristics that define the "species." For example, when he says, "Man is a species-being, not only because in practice and in theory he adopts the species (his own as well as those of other things) as his object" (CW, 3, p. 275), "species" refers to the interactive nature of the members of the species, since without interaction, it would be impossible to adopt one's own species as an object. On the other hand, when Marx says, "It is just in his work upon the objective world, therefore, that man really proves himself to be a species-being. This production is his active species-life" (CW, 3, p. 277), "species" refers to man's ability to act upon nature consciously. Nothing is implied about any social processes through which this might occur.

This example shows that, in reading Marx's early work, close attention must be paid to his precise meaning when he uses "species" (*Gattung*). This is also the case in another respect. As mentioned earlier, the term *Gattung* has synonyms; these synonyms are not considered when *Gattung* is routinely translated as "species." Consider the quote given above. Marx writes that "Man is a species-being, not only because . . . he adopts the species (his own as well as those of other things) as his object." However, "species" when referring to "other things" could better be rendered by "nature of other things." In German, no word distinction must be made since the word *Gattung* (species) can substitute for its synonym *Art* (nature). Thus, if *Gattung* is translated by "species" (as is usually the case), the German synonyms for which "species" could stand must be kept in mind.

Another potential source of confusion is *Gattungswesen*, a word frequently used in Marx's early writings. It is sometimes overlooked in translations that *Wesen* has different meanings in German. For example, *Wesen* can stand for *Sein* (translated by Cassell as being, existence; essence, true nature), "*Dasein*" (translated by Cassell as presence; existence, life), or *Natur* (in the sense of "nature of something") (Paul, 1966). *Wesen* itself is translated by Cassell as reality, substance, essence; being, creature, living thing, organism; state, condition; nature, character, property, intrinsic virtue, and so forth). Thus, when Marx says that man is a species-being (*Gattungswesen*), he refers to the fact that man, in his existence (*Sein, Dasein*), is a member of a species. When he says that man is "estranged from his (*Gattungswesen*)" (CW, 3, p. 277; MEW, EB 1.T., p. 517), he means that man is estranged from the nature of his species. The second meaning is markedly different from the first one; yet, the same word ("*Wesen*") can be used in German to render both meanings. The second meaning, however, is sometimes rendered in English in the same way as the first, usually with "species-being." This is inadequate since, according to Cassell, "being" does not translate into the German *Natur*, but only into *Sein* and *Dasein*.

Not only is the inadequacy of a technical nature, but it also has important consequences in interpreting Marx. We have seen that, for Marx, man is a species-being because of the characteristics by which man differs from the animals and by which human society differs from animal colonies. Based on these characteristics, each human individual is a member of a group of other individuals sharing the same characteristics. The individual exists as a member of a species, and he is a species-being. According to Marx's definition, man is and remains a species-being as long as the defining characteristics remain the same. As long as man, contrary to animals, remains a being endowed with certain faculties, he will remain a species-being. It therefore is misleading to say that man is estranged from his species-being, since, although estranged, he remains man. It is more meaningful to say that man is estranged from his species-nature; that is, he is prevented from using the faculties that are given to him by nature and that define him as a species according to *his* will. Although a member of a species (a species-being), he cannot produce as he wants, and he cannot interact as would be the case if he could produce as he wants. In other words, he is estranged from his species-nature. It would have been more beneficial to translate "estranged from his species-nature" instead of "estranged from his species-being" (CW, 3, p. 277).[3]

Although the vocabulary of the young Marx is often difficult to decipher, it has been possible to show a very strong consistency in his use of terms. Consequently, I cannot endorse Adam Schaff's statement that Marx's early vocabulary "was neither consistent nor precise" (Schaff, 1970a: 84).

There is yet another point of disagreement with Schaff and Fromm. It has been shown that Marx's theory of human nature consists of two clearly delineated components, one of which is based on Marx's biological model and the other on his historical model of human nature. Quoting Fromm, Schaff writes:

> Marx was opposed to two positions: the unhistorical one that the nature of man is a substance present from the very beginning of history, and the relativistic position that man's nature has no inherent quality whatsoever and is nothing but the reflex of social conditions. But he never arrived at the full development of his own theory concerning the nature of man, transcending both the unhistorical and the relativistic positions; hence he left himself open to various and contradictory interpretations" (Schaff, 1970a: 88).

Schaff's position is unjustified because, as Marx himself showed, the unhistorical position is based on criteria that distinguish man from animal. These criteria are not subject to historical change unless, of course, one assumes that man, at the beginning of his evolution, did not possess the characteristics that distinguish him today from animals. When defining human nature, however, Marx does not seem to have been concerned with such matters. Instead, he based his theory on the "human animal" as it is known to us today, assuming that, as far as the history of man is known to us, the defining characteristics have remained unchanged.

From another angle, Israel makes a similar charge against Marx's theory of human nature. He claims that Marx's concept of man "contains metaphysical notions concerning the characteristics which comprise man's essence"(that is, man's nature) and that it is not empirically testable (Israel, 1971: 8-9, 75, 76). According to the presentation of Marx's theory of human nature here, however, one would have to conclude that the characteristics which he specified as distinguishing man from the animals are empirically verifiable and therefore far from metaphysical.

Israel's presentation of Marx's theory of human nature is unclear in another respect. He writes that Marx adopted Schiller's view "that human nature could reach perfection" (Israel, 1971: 24) and that "human nature can be conceived of, on the one hand, as the *potentialities* which mankind has and, on the other hand, as the *existing* human being seen as a consequence of a certain social structure " (Israel, 1971: 57). Here, Israel fails to distinguish between the two components of Marx's theory of human nature. He is likely referring to that part of Marx's theory of human nature that is labeled here as the historical model of human nature. He does not specify, however. It would not be possible to speak of human nature reaching perfection in any other way since it is perfect in its own right, as is shown in the comparison of man with animals. Israel believes that the

> young Marx's theory concerning man's nature contained value premises which were anchored in a specific historical period characterized by specific conditions: it was a situation marked by the transition from the artisan to the industrial level of production. . . . Marx's theory of man as developed in the *Manuscripts* was characterized by romantic ideas and notions concerning the nature of work, which, in my opinion, were influenced by the historical situation preceding the process of industrialization (Israel, 1971: 262).

If my delineation of Marx's theory of human nature is correct, no such conclusion can be drawn, regardless of what model (historical or unhistorical) is considered. First, a comparison of man with the animals does not contain "value premises which were anchored in a specific historical period." Second, any determination of the characteristics of human nature which are historically determined does not depend on particular values, since it is merely based on a comparison of human behavior under various historical conditions. Therefore, if anything depends on value, it is not Marx's theory of human nature but his assumption that man ought to be able to live according to what he thinks is man's nature. Third, as our analysis of Marx's theory of human nature has shown, there is no evidence, contrary to Israel's implied view, that this theory changed as Marx wrote his later works. By selecting passages from Marx's early and later works, it could be shown that his theory of human nature did not change.

In a recent essay, Daniel Bell suggests that Marx was seeking to resolve "a number of inherently irreconcilable dilemmas in the epistemology and sociology of the social sciences" (Bell, 1977: 189). Bell further asserts that one such dilemma is "human nature seen as an essence (*Wesen*) versus human nature seen as recreated by history." Bell is correct in recognizing that Marx's theory of human nature consists of two parts. My analysis above, however, suggests no reason why these two parts should be thought of as irreconcilable opposites; on the contrary, they complement each other. Marx's biological model can determine only those characteristics that distinguish man from animals and that thus define human nature. It cannot, and does not claim to, explain the differences in human behavior (that is, human nature) over time. For this, Marx makes use of an historical model. This and the biological model are mutually exclusive, however, and are not irreconcilable but complementary.

NOTES

1. My translation differs from Martin Nicolaus' translation of the *Grundrisse* insofar as it replaces "that their common species-being (*Gattungswesen*) is acknowledged by all" with "that all know their species-nature (*Gattungswesen*) to be social (*gemeinschaftlich*)"; and "at bottom" with "at bottom (*au fond*)" (see G, p. 243).

2. For additional illustration, consider the following quotes:

But also when I am active *scientifically*, etc.—an activity which I can seldom perform in direct community with others—then my activity is *social*, because I perform it as a *man*. Not only is the material of my activity given to me as a social product (as is even the language in which the thinker is active): my own existence *is* social activity, and therefore that which I make of myself,

I make of myself for society and with the consciousness of myself as a social being.

My *general* consciousness is only the *theoretical* shape of that of which the *living* shape is the *real* community, the social fabric, although at the present day *general* consciousness is an abstraction from real life and as such confronts it with hostility. The *activity* of my general consciousness, as an activity, is therefore also my *theoretical* existence as a social being.

Above all we must avoid postulating "society" again as an abstraction *vis-a-vis* the individual. The individual *is the social being* . . . man's individual and species-life are not *different*. (CW, 3, p. 298-299; MEW, EB 1.T., p. 538).

Language, like consciousness, only arises from the need, the necessity, of intercourse with other men. Where there exists a relationship, it exists for me. (CW, 5, p. 44; MEW, 3, p. 30).

In a sort of way, it is with man as with commodities. Since he comes into the world neither with a looking glass in his hand, nor as a Fichtian philosopher, to whom "I am I" is sufficient, man first sees and recognises himself in other men. Peter only establishes his own identity as a man by first comparing himself with Paul as being of like kind. And thereby Paul, just as he stands in his Pauline personality, becomes to Peter the type of the genus homo (C1, p. 59; MEW, 23, p. 67).

3. Marx himself (CW, 3, p. 277; MEW, EB, 1.T., p. 517) explains that estrangement from *Gattungswesen* means estrangement from "species-nature." In the *Collected Works* (Vol. 3, p. 277), the translation is not consistent.

Marx makes another use of *Gattungswesen* or *Gattungssein*: "the *divine* power of money lies in its *character* as men's estranged, alienating and self-disposing *species-nature*" (*Gattungswesen*) (CW, 3, p. 325; MEW, EB 1.T., p. 565). Here *Gattungswesen* refers not to the species' principal nature, but to its nature as it applies to a certain historical situation. The word *Gattungswesen* is used in conjunction with Marx's historical model of human nature rather than the biological one.

3

Estrangement: The Consequences of Being Coerced into Selling One's Labor Power

Before it can be shown how Marx's theory of estrangement derives directly from his concept of human nature, we must first examine how Marx perceived some other aspects of social life. This examination will then be helpful in understanding Marx's theory of estrangement.

Throughout his work, Marx emphasized that, although some individuals may have some choice as to the persons or institutions to which they sell their labor power, under a system of wage labor it is capital that commands labor. The observation that capital has more power than labor is manifest by the fact that the capitalist as the agent of capital has more alternatives than the worker.

> Wages are determined through the antagonistic struggle between capitalist and worker. Victory goes necessarily to the capitalist. The capitalist can live longer without the worker than can the worker without the capitalist (CW, 3, p. 235); MEW, EB 1.T., p. 471).

> . . . it is just the capacity of the capitalist to direct his capital into another channel which either renders the worker, who is restricted to some particular branch of labour, destitute, or forces him to submit to every demand of this capitalist (CW, 3, p. 236; MEW, EB 1.T., p. 472).

Marx was even more distressed by capital's apparent power to seriously threaten even the worker's physical survival:

> [T]he *worker* has the misfortune to be a *living* capital, and therefore an *indigent capital,* one which loses its interest, and hence its livelihood, every moment it is not working. . . . As soon, therefore, as it occurs to capital (whether from necessity or caprice) no longer to be for the worker, he himself is no longer for himself: he has *no* work, hence *no* wages, and since he has no existence *as a human being* but only *as a worker,* he can go and bury himself, starve to death, etc (CW, 3, p. 283; MEW, EB 1.T., p. 523).

> [I]n those cases where worker and capitalist equally suffer, the worker suffers in his very existence, the capitalist in the profit on his dead mammon (CW, 3, p. 237; MEW, EB 1.T., p. 473).

In view of such an account of the power of capital, we should not be surprised by Marx's categoric statement that "Capital is thus the *governing power* over labour" (CW, 3, p. 247; MEW, EB 1.T., p. 484). However, the agents of capital—the capitalists—do not possess this governing power on the basis of personal or human qualities, but merely because they *own* capital with its inherent power to purchase anything and everything. The capitalist's power "is the purchasing power of his capital, which nothing can withstand" (CW, 3, p. 247). Thus, whereas in earlier societies people were herded together to engage in forced labor, capital manages to accomplish the same coordination of labor power through the exchange of free labor (MEW, G, p. 427).

Capital represents

> a coercive relation, which compels the working class to do more work than the narrow round of its own life-wants prescribes. As a producer of the activity of others, as a pumper-out of surplus-labour and exploiter of labour-power, it surpasses in energy, disregard of bounds, recklessness and efficiency, all earlier systems of production based on directly compulsory labour (C1, p. 293; MEW, 23, p. 328).

Capital not only governs labor in society as a whole, but also has command over labor during the act of production. "Personified capital, the capitalist takes care that the labourer does his work satisfactorily (*ordentlich*) and with the proper degree of intensity" (C1, p. 293; MEW, 23, p. 328; translation mine).

At first, it may appear that the worker is a free agent and that capital is not coercive. Indeed, the worker himself sells his labor power to the capitalist and engages in a contractual relationship with him. After the deal is made, however, it is discovered that the worker

> Was no "free agent," that the time for which he is free to sell his labour-power is the time for which he is forced to sell it, that in fact the vampire will not lose its hold on him "so long as there is a muscle, a nerve, a drop of blood to be exploited" (C1, p. 285; MEW, 23, p. 319).[1]

In fact, the worker was in the bondage of capital even before he appeared as a "free agent" of his labor power. As part of an unending cycle, all he can do is sell his labor power over and over again. It is the capitalist process of production itself which, based on the fact that the worker does not own his product of labor, "incessantly hurls back the labourer on to the market as a vendor of his labour-power, and that incessantly converts his own product into a means by which another man can purchase him" (C1, pp. 541-542; MEW, 23, p. 603). The capitalist process of production incessantly forces the worker "to sell his labour-power in order to live, and enables the capitalist to purchase labour-power in order that he may enrich himself" (C1, p. 541; MEW, 23, p. 603). This process keeps the worker in constant bondage, and in the case of child labor, even the formality of a voluntary sale disappears (MEW, 23, p. 603).

WAGE LABOR: THE COERCION TO GIVE UP ONE'S WILL AND CONTROL OVER ONE'S BODY

In return for his continued physical existence, the worker is compelled to repeatedly sell his labor power as one would sell any other commodity. *But since labor power cannot in reality be separated from the locus of this power—a human being with distinct qualities and needs—the individual as the locus of labor power is also treated as any other commodity.* Not only does capital coerce the individual to become a commodity in that he or she is forced to sell his labor power, but also once the labor is sold, the individual worker possessing this power loses control over it. Once sold, labor power is the property of capital, property for which the locus of this power (the worker) receives a sum of money in return. However, labor power cannot become the property of capital without the locus of this power, for the time contracted, also becoming the property of capital. As is the case with any other commodity, the capitalist owner of labor power has the right to subject this power to *his* will. Having this right, however, implies that the individual, who is the source of labor power, no longer is allowed to exert his/her will over their own power, since the individual cannot be separated from the labor power he/she puts out. If labor power becomes a commodity so must the individual putting out this labor power.

The worker is thus forced (1) to sell his labor power and (2) to give up his command over it once it is sold. Even if the terms of employment are attractive, this principal condition does not change. Thus, Marx writes: "The raising of wages excites in the worker the capitalists' mania to get rich, which he, however, can only satisfy by the sacrifice of his mind and body" (CW, 3, p. 238; MEW, EB 1.T., p. 474). And since the worker is forced to become a commodity by being coerced into selling his labor power as if it were any other commodity and giving up his control over it once it has been sold, the stage is set for him to be treated as a thing, as a machine with the capacity to perform certain tasks and also subject to the owner's will. "Since the worker has sunk to the level of a machine, he can be confronted by the machine as a competitor" (CW, 3, p. 238).

The worker therefore serves a will that is not his own. Furthermore, he is treated as a commodity and, like a machine, acts in behalf of a will outside himself. This is not the case if the worker is not coerced into selling his labor power. "So far as the labour-process is purely individual," writes Marx,

one and the same labourer writes in himself all the functions, that later on become separated. When an individual appropriates natural objects for his livelihood, no one controls him but himself. Afterwards he is controlled by others. A single man cannot operate nature without calling his own muscles into play under the control of his own brain. As in the natural body head and hand wait upon each other, so the labour-process unites the labour of the hand with that of the head. Later on they part company and even become deadly foes" (C1, p. 476; MEW, 23, p. 531).

And in the *Grundrisse,* Marx says that

> in the production process of capital labour is a totality—a combination
> of labours—whose individual component parts are alien to one another,
> so that the overall process as a totality is *not* the *work* of the individual
> worker, and is furthermore the work of the different workers together
> only to the extent that they are (forcibly) combined, and do not (volun-
> tarily) enter into combination with one another. The combination of
> this labour appears just as subservient to and led by an alien will and an
> alien intelligence—leaving its *animating unity* elsewhere . . . " (G, p. 470;
> MEW, G, pp. 374-375).

In summary, it may be noted that under capital, unlike slavery, "the
worker is not a condition of production, only work is" (G, p. 498). That
is, only the cost of labor power is considered in the decision-making processes of the agents of capital. The fact that the individual, as the locus
of this power, also has needs remains ignored. In addition, capital coerces
the worker by appropriating his will: "The presupposition of the master-
servant relation is the appropriation of an alien *will*. . . ," and this relation
is "reproduced—in mediated form—in capital" (G, pp. 500-501; MEW, G,
p. 400).

In order to elaborate on the fact that coercion alone makes wage labor
possible, it will be fruitful to examine the parallels Marx sees between wage
labor and other forms of coerced labor resulting in slavery, serfdom, and
the like.

Insofar as wage labor is subject to an alien will it resembles slavery: "A
man is continually compelled to sell his labour-power, i.e., himself to another
man . . ." (C2, p. 444; MEW, 24, p. 438). Marx's analogies to slavery further
illustrate this point:

> The Roman slave was held by fetters: The wage labourer is bound to his
> owner by invisible threads (C1, p. 538; MEW, 23, p. 599).

> The essential difference between the various economic forms of society,
> between, for instance, a society based on slave labour, and one based on
> wage labour, lies only in the mode in which this surplus-labour is in each
> case extracted from the actual producer, the labourer (C1, p. 209; MEW,
> 23, p. 231; see also MEW, 24, p. 385).

The more they [the workers] wish to earn, the more must they sacrifice their time and carry out slave-labour, completely losing all their freedom, in the service of greed (CW, 3, p. 237; MEW, EB 1.T., p. 473).[2]

The analogy between wage labor and slavery is an apt one. Engels concisely summed up some of the parallels between wage labor and slavery, showing that the slave can have a better existence than the worker, since the slave's biological existence is guaranteed, while the worker's is not. A slave is the property of his master, who has an interest in keeping his slave producing; the worker is *forced* to sell his labor power on a daily and hourly basis. However, the worker's labor power is purchased only when it is needed; consequently, the worker's existence is threatened. Capitalism secures only the existence of the proletariat as a class, and not the existence of the individual worker (Engels, MEW, 4, p. 366).

Man under capital is forced to sell his labor power and is forced to subordinate his will to an alien will; as Marx's analogies with slavery point out, this condition is tantamount to slavery. The difference is that under capital slavery is a mediated form of slavery while, earlier, slavery was based on direct domination. Armed with this knowledge as well as knowledge of Marx's theory of human nature, it is now possible to address the question of estrangement. As will be apparent, Marx's theory of estrangement rests directly on the postulates outlined so far.

THE CONSEQUENCES OF BEING COERCED
INTO SELLING ONE'S LABOR POWER

Under capital, the worker is forced to sell his labor power in return for a wage, which then allows him to purchase commodities necessary for his sustenance. The worker then does not produce his sustenance directly. Nor does he own the means to do so. He is thus forced to sell his only asset—his labor power. According to Marx, this process implies that the original connection of the means of production with the individual exerting labor power has been dissolved. As a result, "the mass of the people, the labourers, have, as non-owners, come face to face with the non-labourers as the owners of these means of production" (C2, p. 31; MEW, 24, p. 38).[3] The workers not only lack the means to transform and manipulate nature in the process of production, but they also have no claim to the product of their labor. They produce the product for and in behalf of an alien will.

For the labor power expended, they are compensated not with the product of their labor but with a sum of money, a wage. Marx therefore concludes that the worker is estranged in two principal ways. He who is coerced into selling his labor power, and labor under the domination of an alien will is estranged from (1) the product of his labor, and (2) the act of production.

ESTRANGEMENT FROM THE PRODUCT OF ONE'S LABOR

As shown earlier, man differs from the animals in being a conscious being, and on the basis of such criteria Marx determines what human nature is. The criteria themselves, if they are to determine in an ahistorical way what human nature is, are derived from a comparison of man with animals. Thus, unlike animals, man by nature is able to confront his product of labor freely, while the animal's product belongs immediately to its physical body (CW, 3, pp. 276-277). The nature of man is thus to confront his product of labor freely. Man not only has the natural faculty to make his "life activity itself the object of his will and of his consciousness"(CW, 3, p. 276), but he is also by nature able to confront the product of his labor both consciously and freely. This product, of course, is again an integral part of his environment and, thus, again an object of man's will and conscious life activity. For Marx, then, man has the faculty, given to him by nature, to act consciously upon nature as such as well as upon the products of his labor.

Under capital, man is not allowed to live according to his nature. Since he must sell his labor, his own product of labor ceases to be an object of his will and consciousness. Rather, under capital the product of a worker's labor becomes the object of a will that is alien to him/her. For Marx, this condition is unnatural, for *by nature* the human producer has the faculty to freely and consciously confront the product of his labor and subject it to his will. The capitalist mode of production prevents the producer from subjecting his product of labor to his will as he has by nature the faculty to do. In this context, Marx speaks of the estrangement of man from the product of his labor (CW, 3, p. 274). Referring to the worker, he speaks of "the *estrangement*, the loss of the object, of his product" (CW, 3, p. 273), "the estrangement of the object of labour" (CW, 3, p. 274), and so forth.

The producer's inalienable ability to subject the product of his labor to his own will is denied, and instead, the workers' products are subject to a will alien to the producers, the will of the capitalists who appropriate the product of labor. Hence, the worker cannot dispose of his product. And since it is subject to an alien will, his own product confronts him as "something alien, as a power independent of the producer" (CW, 3, p. 272). This, Marx says, is a fact of political economy (CW, 3, p. 271). While "the product of labour is labour which has been embodied in an object, which has become material," and while "labour's realisation is its objectification," under "these economic conditions this realisation of labour appears as a *loss of realisation* for the workers; objectification as *loss of the object and bondage to it;* appropriation *as estrangement, as alienation"* (CW, 3, p. 272; MEW, EB 1.T., pp. 511-512). To this Marx adds: "So much does the appropriation of the object appear as estrangement that the more objects the worker produces the less he can possess and the more he falls under the sway of his product, capital" (CW, 3, p. 272; MEW, EB 1.T., p. 512).

The greater the worker's product "the less is he himself" (CW, 3, p. 272).

The *alienation* of the worker in his product means not only that his labour becomes an object, an *external* existence, but that it exists *outside him,* independently, as something alien to him, and that it becomes a power on its own confronting him. It means that the life which he has conferred on the object confronts him as something hostile and alien (CW, 3, p. 272; MEW, EB 1.T., p. 512).

The relationship of the worker to the product of his own labor is therefore one in which the worker is dominated by his very own product. This condition goes against the individual's nature, since human beings have the capability to appropriate their own product as well as subject it to their will. The political economy under capitalism forcibly prevents the worker from doing this. Such a political economy is based on processes, although manmade,[4] that result in man not living according to his human nature.

THE WORKER'S ESTRANGEMENT FROM THE ACT OF PRODUCTION AND FROM HIMSELF

Marx asks the following question: "How could the worker come to face the product of his activity as a stranger, were it not that in the very act of production he was estranging himself from himself?" (CW, 3, p. 274;

MEW, EB 1.T., p. 514). He postulates that "in the estrangement of the object of labour is merely summarized the estrangement, the alienation, in the activity of labour itself" (CW, 3, p. 274; MEW, EB 1.T., p. 514).

We have seen that the worker is coerced into selling his labor power and that, once his labor power is sold, he himself becomes subject to an alien will. He is forced to do so because he does not have any other means by which he could produce his livelihood; he does not own any other means but his labor power—that is, he does not own the means of production. In Capital, Marx emphasizes that, historically speaking, individuals "became sellers of themselves only after they had been robbed of all their own means of production" (C1, p. 669; MEW, 23, p. 743). The lack of ownership of the means of production is therefore directly related to wage labor and is the reason why, under capital, the worker is coerced into subordinating himself to an alien will. This same lack is directly related to and expressive of the fact that the worker is prevented from appropriating the product of his own labor, since the means of production are in themselves nothing but the product of labor. Although the worker is the capitalist's "personal source of wealth," he is "devoid of all means of making that wealth his own" (C1, p. 535; MEW, 23, p. 596). The capitalist's personal source of wealth of course, also includes the means of production he owns (see C1, p. 535 and MEW, 23, p. 595). In addition, it is particularly the product of man's labor as represented in the means of production which, subject to an alien will, is turning into an alien power. Capital, constant and variable, confronts the worker "as the *totality of the objective conditions* of labour," "as alien property," and as time proceeds the "conditions of labour confront the individual worker in an ever more gigantic form" (TS 3, pp. 352-353; MEW, 26.3, pp. 344-345).[5] In this context, it is therefore possible to speak of the "alienation of the conditions of production" (TS 3, p. 530; MEW, 26.3, p. 519).

Marx contends, then, that "estrangement from the product of one's labour" is directly connected with man's "estrangement from the act of production." As we have just seen, under "the act of production" one should also understand the "totality of the objective conditions of labour," namely, capital in its constant and variable form. Both forms of estrangement always exist simultaneously.[6] Common to both is their source. A will alien to the worker controls the product of labor, and hence the totality of the conditions of production as well, that is, capital in its constant and variable form.

According to Marx's theory of human nature, man by nature has the ability to make "his life activity itself the object of his will and of his consciousness" (CW, 3, p. 276). Man's species-character is his free and conscious activity (CW, 3, p. 276). Under capitalism, however, the conditions of labor are subject to a will alien to the worker, thus preventing the worker from making work a free and conscious activity. Marx points out that "labour is therefore not voluntary, but coerced; it is *forced labour*" (CW, 3, p. 274). The act of production is one of coercion, outside of the individual worker's control. Thus, the worker is prevented from producing freely and under the guidance of *his* will and consciousness, and is coerced into producing according to a will alien to him. The worker is estranged from the act of production, which is also saying that he is estranged from himself: "[T]he external character of labour for the worker appears in the fact that it is not his own, but someone else's, that it does not belong to him, that in it he belongs, not to himself, but to another" (CW, 3, p. 274; MEW, EB 1.T., p. 514). Man is estranged from himself because his own active functions, his life activity, are not his but someone else's (CW, 3, p. 276). Self-estrangement consists in the fact that the worker's "personal life—for what is life but activity?—is an activity which is turned against him, independent of him and not belonging to him" (CW, 3, p. 275; MEW, EB 1.T., p. 515). Since man's activity is not his own but someone else's, it becomes a mere means. As we have seen, since man is forced to sell his labor power, it becomes a means to "maintain physical existence" (CW, 3, pp. 274-277; MEW, EB 1.T., pp. 514-517).

ESTRANGEMENT FROM NATURE

Like the animals, man depends on nature for his livelihood. However, men begin to distinguish themselves from animals as soon as they begin to *produce* their means of subsistence, a step which is conditioned by their physical organisation. By producing their means of subsistence men are indirectly producing their material life" (CW, 5, p. 31; MEW, 3, p. 21). Man manipulates nature; he does not merely live off it. He also manipulates nature consciously. Hence, the best of bees differ from the worst architect by the fact that

the architect raises his structure in imagination before he erects it in reality. At the end of every labour-process, we get a result that already

existed in the imagination of the labourer at its commencement. He
not only effects a change of form in the material on which he works,
but he also realises a purpose of his own. (C1, p. 174; MEW, 23, p. 193).

Consciousness also allows man to produce "free from need," "in accordance
with the laws of beauty," (CW, 3, pp. 276-277), and so on.

The link to nature is cut if workers, against their natural ability, are prevented from manipulating nature according to their will and consciousness,
and if in the act of production man is forced to manipulate nature according
to an alien will, a will independent of the producer. This point is illustrated
in the *Grundrisse*:

> [T]he relation of labour to capital, or to the objective conditions of
> labour as capital, presupposes a process of history which dissolves the
> various forms in which the worker is a proprietor, or in which the pro-
> prietor works. Thus above all (1) *Dissolution* of the relation to the earth—
> land and soil—as natural condition of production—to which he relates
> as his own inorganic being; the workshop of his forces, and the domain
> of his will (translation mine).[7]

When the link to nature is not broken, nature is man's inorganic body. Under
conditions in which man is *not* forced to produce under an alien will, "man's
physical and spiritual life is linked to nature" (CW, 3, p. 276). But under
capitalism this is not the case. Marx speaks of man's estrangement from
nature (CW, 3, pp. 276-277; MEW, EB 1.T., pp. 516-517), which means
that man's "inorganic body, nature, is taken away from him" (CW, 3, p. 277).
As a result, man is also prevented from seeing, through the act of production, nature "as *his* work and his reality" (CW, 3, p. 277). Marx goes so far
as to say that even man's advantage over animals is transformed insofar as
"his inorganic body, nature, is taken away from him" (CW, 3, p. 277).

ESTRANGEMENT FROM THE SPECIES AND FROM MAN

In the earlier discussion of Marx's concept of species, it is concluded
that the same characteristics differentiating each individual from animals
also designate the nature of the species. In this sense, the human species
consists of individuals sharing the same biological characteristics, those
characteristics that also define human nature. Beyond that, however, it is
shown that the way in which human individuals interact also defines the

species. Hence, human interaction is by nature very different from animal interaction, particularly when it comes to production. For instance, the "need on the part of one can be satisfied by the product of the other. . . , and . . . the one is capable of producing the object of the need of the other" (G, p. 243; MEW, G, p. 154). According to Marx, this capability is qualitatively very different from that of animals. The species-nature is defined by the biological nature of human individuals comprising it, as well as by the quality of interaction among these individuals.

When Marx says that "estranged labour estranges the *species* from man" (CW, 3, p. 276), he does not mean that man ceases to be a member of the species. Rather, man remains a member of his species by definition. Under capital, however, the species as a whole is prevented from living according to its natural capability. The individual is therefore prevented from being a member of a "group" (species) which is allowed to pursue life according to its natural capability.

Marx maintains that "productive life is the life of the species" and that "free, conscious activity is man's species-character" (CW, 3, p. 276). If, however, as is the case under capitalism, man is forced to produce under an alien will and is prevented from appropriating the product of his own labor, the species loses its species character, and individuals, although capable, are prevented from interacting in such a way that the "need on the part of one can be satisfied by the product of the other." Man is estranged from the species. He is forced to interact with other members of the species in a way that goes against the species' natural abilities, since, to the worker, an alien will determines what is produced, and how and for whom something is produced: "estranged labour . . . changes for him [i.e., man] the *life of the species* into a means of individual life. . . . In tearing away from man the object of his production, therefore, estranged labour tears from him his *species-life,* his real objectivity as a member of the species" (CW, 3, pp. 276-277; MEW, EB 1.T., pp. 516-517). Estranged labor thus makes "man's species-life a means to his physical existence" (CW, 3, p. 277). It "estranges the life of the species and individual life, and . . . makes individual life in its abstract form the purpose of the life of the species, likewise in its abstract and estranged form" (CW, 3, p. 276; MEW, EB 1.T., p. 516).[8]

The form of human interaction under capital and wage labor is therefore quite different from what it could be according to the species-nature. Species membership becomes a mere formality, and interaction in productive life (species-life) a mere means to sustain physical existence. For

Marx, it is very obvious that "the proposition that man's species-nature is estranged from him means that one man is estranged from the other" (CW, 3, p. 277; MEW, EB 1.T., p. 517). At yet another place he states:

An immediate consequence of the fact that man is estranged from the product of his labour, from his life activity, from his species-nature is the *estrangement of man* from *man*. When man confronts himself, he confronts the *other* man. What applies to a man's relation to his work, to the product of his labour and to himself, also holds of a man's relation to the other man, and to the other man's labour and object of labour (translation mine; MEW, EB 1.T., pp. 517-518).[9]

In the *Grundrisse,* Marx reiterates this conclusion when he states that universal production on the basis of exchange value "produces . . . the alienation of the individual from himself and others" (G, p. 162; MEW, G, p. 80).

ESTRANGEMENT OF THE CAPITALIST

Here we consider the question as to whether nonworkers—those who are not engaged in production—are also estranged. First, we must remind ourselves that, although the workers are subject to an alien will and power, that will and power is mediated by other human beings. "If my own activity does not belong to me," asks Marx, "if it is an alien, a coerced activity, to whom, then, does it belong?" His answer is that it belongs "to a being other than myself." "The *alien* being to whom labour and the product of labour belongs, in whose service labour is done and for whose benefit the product of labour is provided, can only be *man* himself" (CW, 3, p. 278; MEW, EB 1.T., p. 518). Capitalists, as the human agents of capital, are also the human agents of the alien power controlling the workers. As members of the nonworking class and subject to constraints such as competition, they represent the alien will to which the workers are subjected. Since the worker is continually forced to resell his labor power to capital, he continually renews his estrangement through his activity which is compelled to follow an alien will. Of course, the capitalist is not compelled to sell his labor for an existence, but he, too, is a member of the species, and his human nature is the same as that of others. Although not forced to sell his labor power, the capitalist is still not a free agent, and, as we have seen, is compelled to live in a situation in which man is estranged from man. Since the workers are prevented from interacting with others in such ways as their human nature enables them, their interaction with the agents of capital is also marked by estrangement. From the capitalists' point of view, this estrangement is not the result of their own labor activity, as is the case with workers. It is merely a condition that confronts them as a result of their relationship with the workers. Marx elaborates this point when he says:

> First it has to be noted that everything which appears in the worker as an *activity of alienation, of estrangement,* appears in the non-worker as a *state of alienation, of estrangement. . . .* Secondly, . . . the worker's *real, practical attitude* in production and to the product (as a state of mind) appears in the non-worker confronting him as a *theoretical* attitude" (CW, 3, p. 282; MEW, EB 1.T., p. 522).

Although both worker and capitalist are estranged, the estrangement, because of differences in the social position, has a different impact on the two groups. As Marx writes in *The Holy Family:*

> The propertied class and the class of the proletariat present the same human self-estrangement. But the former class feels at ease and strengthened in this self-estrangement, it recognises estrangement as *its own power* and has in it the *semblance* of a human existence. The latter feels annihilated in estrangement; it sees in it its own powerless-ness and the reality of an inhuman existence (CW, 4, p. 36; MEW, 2, p. 37).

While the capitalist's existence resembles a human existence, it is never-theless not what it could be according to the nature of man and the species.

THE CAPITALIST'S RELATIONSHIP TO THE WORKER

As already indicated, "the *capitalist,* as capitalist, is simply the personifi-cation of capital, the creation of labour with its own will and personality which stands in opposition to labour" (TS 3, p. 296; MEW, 26.3, p. 290). It must be kept in mind, however, that for capital to be capital and for the capitalist to be a capitalist, the capitalist must not only possess money. He must simultaneously have a social situation in which the means and conditions of production are separated from those who produce. Thus, Marx says that

> it is not the ownership of money which makes the capitalist a capitalist. For money to be transformed into capital, the prerequisites for capitalist production must exist, whose first historical presupposition is that separation. The separation, and therefore the existence of the means of labour as capital, is given in capitalist production; this separation which constantly reproduces itself and expands, is the foundation of production (TS 3, p. 272; MEW, 26.3, p. 267).

Given the separation of the means and conditions of production from the worker, money can assume the form of capital; through the capitalist as an agent, money in its historically new form is now capable of employing labor. "Capital *employs* labour," writes Marx, and "the *means of production,* the material conditions of labour" (all various forms of capital) are not subsumed by the worker, "but he is a means for them" (TS 1, p. 390; MEW, 26.1, p. 366). On the other hand, the capitalist as the agent of capital, contrary to previous noncapitalist forms of production, "does not rule over the labourer through any personal qualities he may have, but only insofar as he is 'capital'; his domination is only that of materialised labour over living labour, of the labourer's product over the labourer himself" (TS 1, p. 390; MEW, 26.1, p. 366).

To say that the capitalist is "only capital personified" and that "his soul is the soul of capital" (C1, p. 224) is to imply that the capitalist himself is under certain constraints, and therefore not a free agent himself, since "capital has one single life impulse, the tendency to create value and surplus-value, to make its constant factor, the means of production, absorb the greatest possible amount of surplus-labour" (C1, p. 224; MEW, 23, p. 247). Despite the fact that the capitalist as a person is motivated by the opportunity to retain and consume surplus value (see MEW, 24, p. 387), the capitalist's actions are constrained by the free competition which "brings out the inherent laws of capitalist production, in the shape of external coercive laws having power over every individual capitalist" (C1, p. 257; MEW, 23, p. 286). If, under capital, human life is treated recklessly, it is the result of the total conditions under which capital operates and competes. "Hence," Marx says, "capital is reckless of the health or length of life of the labourer, unless forced by society not to be reckless" (translation mine;[10] MEW, 23, p. 285). With regard to the recklessness of capital, he asserts that "looking at things as a whole, all this does not, indeed, depend on the good or ill will of the individual capitalist" (C1, p. 257; MEW, 23, p. 286).

A COMMENT ON MARX'S TERMINOLOGY: *ENTÄUSSERUNG, ENTFREMDUNG,* ALIENATION

The word "alienation" is often used as the translation of the German words *Entäusserung* and *Entfremdung.* However, use of this word is not consistent. In the *Collected Works, Entfremdung* tends to be rendered by the English word "estrangement," while *Entäusserung* is usually translated as "alienation." This is exemplified by the sentence "In the estrangement (*Entfremdung*) of the object of labour is merely summarised the estrangement (*Entfremdung*), the alienation (*Entäusserung*), in the activity of labour itself" (CW, 3, p. 274; MEW, EB 1.T., p. 514). Yet, the Progress Publishers edition of *Theories of Surplus-Value* and *Capital* (C3, p. 85; MEW, 25, p. 95) renders *Entfremdung* by the word "alienation," as exemplified by "This alienation (*Entfremdung*) of the conditions of production corresponds . . ." (TS 3, pp. 296, 530; MEW, 26.3, pp. 290, 519). Similarly, Nicolaus, in Marx's *Grundrisse,* translates *Entfremdung* with "alienation," while at another place translating *Entäusserung* with "dispossession" (G, pp. 150, 160-162, 674; MEW, G, pp. 68, 78-80, 566).

We will now consider what German words Marx used to convey the terms "alienation." While a few examples will have to suffice in this short space, they are sufficiently representative to allow an opinion on the subject. There seems to be evidence that Marx used the term to mean primarily, and possibly exclusively, the German word *Entäusserung.* Marx translates alienation in James Stuart's sentence "Labour, which through its alienation creates a universal equivalent, I call *industry*" (CPE, p. 58) with the word *Entäusserung* (MEW, 13, p. 44). In the *Grundrisse* Marx also uses the English word "alienation" interchangeably with and to designate the German word *Entäusserung* (MEW, G, pp. 722-723).

Because money is the *general equivalent, the general power of purchasing,* everything can be bought, everything may be transformed into money. But it can be transformed into money only by being alienated (*alieniert*), because the owner alienates (*entäussert*) himself from it.

Everything is therefore alienable, or indifferent for the individual, external to him. Thus the so-called *inalienable (unveräusserlichen), eternal* possessions, and the immovable, solid property relations corresponding to them, break down in the face of money (translation mine). [When "alienation" renders a German word, the particular German word was put in parentheses. "Everything is therefore alienable" is Marx's own sentence.]

Since there is a discrepancy in the ways in which Marx and some translators used the term "alienation," it is important to see whether and how these differences can be reconciled. The above quotation shows that Marx uses *Entäusserung* and *Veräusserung* (or their derivatives) interchangeably. Both words can describe the situation in which somebody divests (*veräussert, entäussert*) himself of something, be it property in the form of a thing, land, or one's labor power. Marx predominantly uses *Entäusserung*, not *Veräusserung*, to describe this situation and, as we have seen, translates it with the word "alienation."

A well-known Latin-German dictionary of 1844 (Freund), translates the Latin word *alienatio* with *Veräusserung* and *Entäusserung*. It adds that, figuratively speaking, *alienatio* can also be translated as *Entfremdung, Sichentfernen von jemandem, Abfall, Abneigung*. The verb *alieno* is similarly translated by this dictionary. Although Marx did use the word *Entfremdung* in the *Grundrisse* and the word *fremd* often throughout his work, he did not apparently use the term "alienation," or any derivative thereof, to mean the German words *Entfremdung* or *fremd*. He did, however, use the term to translate the nonfigurative words *Entäusserung* and *Veräusserung*.

Since Marx used the word *Entäusserung* to render the English "alienation," it will be useful to consult a Latin-English dictionary for its rendering on the word *alienatio*. Based on the Freund Latin-German edition of 1844, an English edition appeared in 1854 (Andrews), thus indicating how the terms *alienatio* and *alieno* were understood then. In this work, *alienatio* is (1) the transferring of the possessions of a thing to another, so as to make it his property; (2) the transferring of one's self, that is, the going over to another; a separation, desertion. Unlike the German, no distinction is made between figurative and nonfigurative speech, although the conveyed meanings are the same. *Alieno* is defined in this way: (1) To make one person another; to make something the property of another; to alienate, to transfer by sale; to remove, to separate, to make foreign;

(2) (referring to the second rendering of *alienatio*) to withdraw or remove anyone from friendship for or love to anyone, to alienate, estrange, set at variance, to make enemies. Again, no differentiation between figurative and nonfigurative speech is made.

It can therefore be concluded that it is not incorrect to translate both *Entäusserung* and *Entfremdung* as "alienation," but that such a rendering is not optimal. Hence, *Entfremdung* should be translated as "estrangement" and *Entäusserung* as "alienation" (see also Schacht, 1971: 80-81), for Marx himself seemed to have reserved the term "alienation" for *Entäusserung* (Andrews, 1854). There is another reason that would strongly support a differentiation between the two terms. While it is possible to "transfer the possession of a thing to another," it does not follow that this *Entäusserung* ("alienation") designates estrangement (*Entfremdung*). Marx is objecting to a very particular alienation (*Entäusserung*), namely, that which allows the previous owner of a thing to be affected in a way that is beyond his control. Thus, Marx assumes that it is human nature, if not interfered with, to satisfy the needs of one individual with the product of another. On this basis, Marx sees human interaction as qualitatively different from that of animals. However, Marx also assumes that it is human nature to alienate (*entäussern*) a thing such that another individual's needs may be satisfied, since otherwise all the products would have to be consumed by the producer and could not become the property of another in order that *the other's* needs may be satisfied. Under capital, the conditions are quite different. First, labor power is alienated, as a result of which the worker also loses control over his product. Second, since he is coerced into selling his labor power and loses control over the products of his labor, his own product confronts him as an object that is subject to another's will, an alien will. The producer is estranged (*entfremdet*) from his product because he was forced to alienate (*entäussern*) his labor power in return for a wage and the abandonment of control over his product of labor.

It can now be easily seen why a clear distinction should be made between *Entäusserung* and *Entfremdung*. Although for Marx they are not mutually exclusive,[11] under such social forms as exist, for example, under capital, *Entäusserung* can and must exist if man is to live according to his nature. Marx's vision of communism therefore consists of a society in which products are mutually produced and consumed without permitting anyone to become an alien power over anyone.[12]

NOTES

1. In this respect, it is important to note that Marx promoted a daily limit on working hours. He urged the workers to unite and to push through the appropriate legislation in the form of a class action.

2. Other passages make the same point:

> What does the primitive accumulation of capital, i.e., its historical genesis, resolve itself into? In so far as it is not immediate transformation of slaves and serfs into wage-labourers, and therefore a mere change of form, it only means the expropriation of the immediate producers, i.e., the dissolution of private property based on the labour of its owner (C1, p. 713; MEW, 23, p. 789).

> The wage-slave, just like the real slave, cannot become a creditor's slave due to his position. (C3, p. 595; MEW, 25, p. 609).

In *Theories of Surplus Value* and *Grundrisse,* Marx also compares slavery and wage labor, stating that wage labor is based on domination mediated through the market, while slavery or other forms of forced labor are based on direct domination of one part of the society by the other (MEW, 26.3, p. 391; MEW, G, p. 655).

3. Consider also the following quote: "The process, therefore, that clears the way for the capitalist system, can be none other than the process which takes away from the labourer the possession of his means of production." (C1, p. 668; MEW, 23, p. 742).

4. In chapters 5, 6, and 8 I discussed Marx's comments on how human beings ever managed to start a process that by its very nature became a detriment to them and prevented them from living according to their inalienable nature.

5. "Conditions of labour" (*Arbeitsbedingungen*) may not adequately convey the meaning of the German word. *Arbeitsbedingungen* are the conditions under which labor is performed. "Conditions," however, stands for *all* parameters to which labor is subject.

6. Since, before entering on the process, his own labour has already been alienated from himself by the sale of his labour-power, has been appropriated by the capitalist and incorporated with capital, it must, during the process, be realised in a product that does not belong to him. Since the process of production is also the process by which the capitalist consumes labour-power, the product of the labourer is incessantly converted, not only into commodities, but into capital, into value that sucks up the value-creating power, into means of subsistence that buy the person of the labourer, into means of production that command the producers (C1, p. 535; MEW, 23, p. 596).

7. "To which he relates as his own inorganic being" is rendered in the Nicolaus translation as "to which he relates as to his own inorganic being" (G, p. 497). See also Marx's use of the word "inorganic" in the *Manuscripts* where he seems to use it as an adjective to nature outside man's organic body (MEW, EB 1.T., pp. 515-

516). The same is the case for other passages in the *Grundrisse* (MEW, G, pp. 375, 384-390).

> "[N]atural conditions of production" includes also any raw materials contained on the planet earth (MEW, G, p. 384).

For further elaboration, consider the following passages:

> Another presupposition is the separation of free labour from the objective conditions of its realization—from the means of labour and the material for labour. Thus, above all, release of the worker from the soil as his natural workshop— hence dissolution of small, free landed property as well as of communal land-ownership resting on the oriental commune (G, p. 471; MEW, G, p. 375).

> It is not the *unity* of living and active humanity with the natural, inorganic conditions of their metabolic exchange with nature, and hence their appropriation of nature, which requires explanation or is the result of an historic process, but rather the *separation* between these inorganic conditions of human existence and this active existence, a separation which is completely posited only in relation of wage labour and capital. In the relations of slavery and serfdom this separation does not take place;" (G, p. 489; MEW, G, p. 389).

8. Here I disagree with Giddens (1971: 15-16) and Petrović who makes a similar argument (1967: 147). Giddens suggests that estrangement from the species must be seen as "a separation from socially generated characteristics and propensities." Capitalism, he maintains, has created a potential which, if realized, could bring about Marx's envisioned society. Such a realization is constantly being frustrated under capitalism, and estrangement is the result.

According to the interpretation given in this study, for Marx estrangement is *not* the frustrated realization of a potential created by the historical mode of production known to us as capitalism. On the contrary, it may be called the frustrated ability (that is, the inability) to live according to what is human nature—not potential, but factual and empirically verifiable human nature.

Giddens assumes his position in part to avoid and warn against an interpretation that postulates that estrangement results from a separation from what might be called a "state of nature." Such a postulate may imply certain assumptions concerning man's goodness, intelligence, creativity, and the like. Clearly, Marx did not believe that estrangement resulted from civilization preventing man from living according to a "state of nature." Still, Marx holds that estrangement results from the inability to live according to one's nature. This nature is defined by means of an empirical comparison with animals, and not by projection in the sense that social theorists sometimes have projected a "state of nature." In his concept of "human nature in general," there is no nostalgia or anything that might be viewed as historically relative. Hence, Marx's "human nature in general" cannot be compared with theories on a state of nature postulated by a Rousseau or Hobbes. Giddens does not make this mistake, but in avoiding it he neglects to see that estrangement results when man is prevented from living according to his nature.

Giddens' interpretation of Marx's theory of estrangement is problematic in other ways as well. How can estrangement be the frustrated realization of a socially created potential if it is a precondition for the development of this potential? As will become evident later, all development of the productive powers of man is seen to occur at the expense of estrangement. Only after sufficient development has occurred does Marx see a society without estrangement (communism) as realizable. He gives a partial modification of this position for the case of Russia; see his letter to Sassulitsch (MEW, 19, p. 242) and the preface to the second Russian edition of the *Manifesto* (MEW, 4, pp. 575-576). Estrangement, however, existed in Marx's view long before the capitalistic foundations for communism were laid. The period of primitive accumulation may be cited as an example. During this period, wage labor was becoming more universal, and, although Marx would not claim that the foundations for communism had been laid by that time, it can be shown that the wage labourer could subject neither his labor power nor the product of his labor to his own will. In short, he was estranged.

9. "Species-nature" is my translation of *Gattungswesen*. See my discussion on pp. 17-22; see also CW, 3, p. 277.

10. The Progress Publishers edition translates *wo es nicht durch die Gesellschaft zur Rücksicht gezwungen wird* as "unless under compulsion from society" (C1, p. 257).

11. At first, it may appear that Marx did not distinguish between *Entäusserung* and *Entfremdung* in the French edition of *Capital,* the translation of which he approved. Thus, "Da vor seinem Eintritt in den Prozess seine eigene Arbeit ihm selbst entfremdet, dem Kapitalisten angeeignet and dem Kapital einverleibt ist," is translated by "Son travail, déjà aliéné, fait propriété du capitaliste et incorporé au capital, même avant que le procès commence. On closer inspection, *entfremdet* here refers to the fact that the worker's labor power is being taken away from him, even before the process of production can begin, to become the property of capital. *Entfremdet* therefore carries the meaning of *entäussert* in the sense that, even before the process of production begins, the worker's labor power has been alienated from him and has been made the property of capital, that is, the property of the capitalist as the agent of capital (MEW, 23, pp. 596-597; *Le Capital:* Livre I, p. 413).

Marx sometimes uses the two words alienation and estrangement in conjunction with each other, merely separating them by a comma. This is nothing but a technique to emphasize that, although the meanings of the two words are different, they are not mutually exclusive under capital (see MEW, EB 1.T., pp. 512, 514, 518, 522).

12. Although I have criticised translations that render *Entfremdung* as "alienation" instead of as "estrangement," whenever quotes from these sources are used, the translation is not changed so that as much authenticity as possible can be preserved. The reader must therefore remember that when sources other than the *Collected Works* are quotes, "alienation" could stand for *Entfremdung*.

4

THE NATURE OF CAPITALIST
SOCIETY AND ECONOMY

In an attempt to review what Marx saw as key elements of capitalism, topics such as surplus value and division of labor must be addressed.

LABOR THEORY OF VALUE, SURPLUS VALUE

A full review of the economic debates in which Marx engaged concerning the labor theory of value is not possible here, nor will I elaborate on what is known today as the "transformation problem." Labor theory of value, surplus value, and exploitation will be defined not in terms of price but in terms of time, as Marx did throughout much of his work. For an account of the principal ways in which he analyzed capitalist society, this procedure will be adequate and not misleading.

Because the worker is forced to sell his labor power and to let it be subject to an alien will, he not only becomes estranged, but also "divests himself (*entäussert sich*) of labour as the force productive of wealth" (G, p. 307).[1] Through this exchange in which the worker receives wages, the capitalist controls the labor of the worker and becomes the owner of the product of labor (see MEW, 23, pp. 199-200). In the *Grundrisse,* Marx writes that the "separation between labour and property in the product of labour, between labour and wealth, is thus posited in this act of exchange itself" (G, p. 307; MEW, G, p. 214). He explicitly postulates that labor is the source of wealth and that, since the product of labor does not belong to the worker, it is the capitalist who appropriates this wealth. The capitalist, of course, does not stockpile his wealth in the form of the product produced by the labor power. The capitalist produces for a market on which he sells the commodities, and in turn, through the medium of money, he accumulates the wealth in the form he desires, be it the means of production or other forms of wealth. In order to accumulate wealth, however, the capitalist must be able to sell his commodities above the cost of production.

Marx assumes that, on the average, commodities are sold above cost. Cost, however, is nothing else but the labor time embodied in a commodity for which the worker is compensated by the particular capitalist, plus the cost of all materials required to produce the commodity. The raw materials in themselves include labor cost and surplus value which one capitalist pays to the other. Generally, an individual capitalist can sell his commodities above cost only if the worker is not fully compensated for the labor performed. Expressed in terms of labor time, it can be said that a particular worker also produces during a certain number of hours without being compensated for this production. The commodities produced during this time are at no labor cost; nevertheless, they are appropriated by the capitalist who can then sell them at whatever price the market will bear. In terms of each particular product, it is therefore possible to say that it contains a portion of labor time for which the worker was not compensated, although he was forced to spend the time in the service of the capitalist as an obligation in return for receiving wages. Marx calls the labor time which the worker performs without compensation *surplus labor*, and compensated labor he calls *necessary labor time*. In the following passage, he summarizes his notions of labor value:

> The value of every commodity is the product of labour; hence this is also true of the value of the product of the annual labour or of the value of society's annual commodity-product. But since all labour resolves itself 1) into necessary labour-time, in which the labourer reproduces merely an equivalent for the capital advanced in the purchase of his labour-power, and 2) into surplus-labour, by which he supplies the capitalist with a value for which the latter does not give any equivalent, hence surplus-value, it follows that all commodity-value can resolve itself only into these two component parts, so that ultimately it forms a revenue for the working-class in the form of

wages, and for the capitalist class in the form of surplus-value. As
for the constant capital-value, i.e., the value of the means of production consumed in the creation of the annual product, it cannot be explained how this value gets into that of the new product (except
for the phrase that the capitalist charges the buyer with it in the sale
of his goods), but ultimately, since the means of production are themselves products of labour, this portion of value can, in turn, consist
only of an equivalent of the variable capital and of surplus-value,
of a product of necessary labour and of surplus-labour. The fact that
the values of these means of production function in the hands of
their employers as capital-values does not prevent them from having
"originally," in the hands of others if we go to the bottom of the matter—even though at some previous time—resolved themselves into the
same two portions of value, hence into two different sources of revenue
. . . the matter presents itself differently in the movement of social
capital, i.e., of the totality of individual capitals, from the way it presents itself for each individual capital considered separately, hence
from the standpoint of each individual capitalist. For the latter the
value of commodities resolves itself into 1) a constant element (a
fourth one, as Adam Smith says), and 2) the sum of wages and surplus-
value, or wages, profit, and rent. But from the point of view of society
the fourth element of Adam Smith, the constant capital-value, disappears (C2, p. 388; MEW, 24, pp. 383-384).

Once the labor theory of value is accepted, that is, once it is recognized
that all wealth and the value of all commodities are a function of the labor
time embodied in it,

the *independent, material form of wealth disappears* and wealth is
shown to be simply the activity of men. Everything which is not the
result of human activity, of labour, is nature, and, as such, is not social
wealth. The phantom of the world of goods fades away and it is seen
to be simply a continually disappearing and continually reproduced
objectivisation of human labor. All solid material wealth is only transi-
tory materialisation of social labour, crystallisation of the production process whose measure is time, the measure of a movement itself.
    The manifold forms in which the various component parts of wealth
are distributed amongst different sections of society lose their apparent

independence. Interest is merely a part of profit, rent is merely surplus profit. Both are consequently merged in profit, which itself can be reduced to *surplus-value,* that is to unpaid labour. The value of the commodity itself, however, can only be reduced to labour-time (TS 3, p. 429; MEW, 26.3, p. 421).

As soon as the postulate that "the value of the commodity itself can only be reduced to labour-time" is accepted, it also becomes clear why both labor and the means of production are continually devalued. Let us consider Marx's argument in *The Poverty of Philosophy,* a work that he repeatedly mentioned in his later writings and that represents the foundation of any of the economic theories which he developed later in his life: "It is important to emphasize the point that what determines value is not the time taken to produce a thing, but the *minimum* time it could possibly be produced in, and this minimum is ascertained by competition" (CW, 6, p. 136; MEW, 4, p. 95). Since the exchange value of a commodity is based on the minimum labor time, the method and means of production used in the production of commodities are subject to constant change. Thus, if the productivity of labor can be augmented sufficiently through the employment of new methods and/or means of production, the previously used means of production may become obsolete (devalued) before its life-span is exhausted. Similarly, without going into the various contingencies of a particular situation, it is possible to say that, since less labor time is required to produce the same commodity if productivity is increased, labor will be less costly (devalued). Here as well competition will bring about a reduction of wages as a result of a greater abundance of workers.

> Competition implements the law according to which the relative value of a product is determined by the labour time needed to produce it. Labour time serving as the measure of marketable value becomes in this way the law of the continual *depreciation* of labour. . . . There will be depreciation not only of the commodities brought into the market, but also of the instruments of production and of whole plants (CW, 6, p. 135; MEW, 4, pp. 94-95).

In view of the fact that labor devalues, that is, that the workers looking for work become more numerous and therefore replaceable as productivity increases, the employer also has less, or no, incentive to protect human life and health. This leads Marx to observe that the capitalist mode of production is wasteful both with respect to human resources and to material means:

> The capitalist mode of production is generally, despite all its niggardliness, altogether too prodigal with its human material, just as, conversely, thanks to its method of distribution of products through commerce and manner of competition, it is very prodigal with its material means, and loses for society what it gains for the individual capitalist (C3, pp. 86-87; MEW, 25, p. 97).

We have seen that according to Marx the capitalist qua capitalist can exist in his competitive world only if he can appropriate enough products of unpaid labor. This surplus value is generally realized and is transformed into the appropriate form of wealth through exchange. The products of labor are exchanged to recover both fixed and variable expense (capital) as well as to obtain additional capital from the surplus product produced by unpaid labor. Since, under capital, the products of labor are produced for a market, in contrast to personal use by the capitalist or the worker, exchange is of prime importance to the capitalist. Only through exchange can he recover his outlays in constant and variable capital as well as obtain additional capital from the surplus product appropriated. The capitalist, then, produces for exchange, he produces commodities (*Waren*) in contrast to only use value. He produces for the exchange value[2] of a particular thing, not for its use value. The capitalist produces only commodities, things which in exchange will yield sufficient money, because only through exchange can he both recover his original capital outlays and obtain additional capital. This is not to say that the commodities produced do not also have use value. They obviously do since it is through exchange that individuals satisfy their needs and that, under capital, individuals obtain those products of labor (commodities) that will be of use to them (see MEW, 23, pp. 55, 57, 62; C1, pp. 48, 50, 54). The capitalists' interest is in the exchange value of commodities, as opposed to their use value, since it is only through exchange and the value obtained therein that the capitalist can recover his additional outlays and enlarge his original capital. When Marx discusses exchange in general, he says that "what . . . concerns producers when they make an exchange, is the question, how much of some other product they get for their own? in what proportions the products are exchangeable?" (C1, p. 79; MEW, 23, p. 89). This observation is equally applicable for the capitalist, who depends on the exchange of his commodities in order to obtain, through the medium of money, the commodities he requires for his own personal consumption as well as for continuing his process of accumulation.

In summary, it can be said that , under capital, things of use value are exchanged and through this exchange obtain an exchange value. Once things of use value are being exchanged and produced for exchange they are commodities. Commodities contain both a use value and an exchange value. Concerning the distinction between the two kinds of value, Marx notes:

> A thing can be of use-value, without having value. This is the case whenever its utility to man is not due to labour. Such are air, virgin soil, natural meadows, etc. A thing can be useful, and the product of human labour, without being a commodity. Whoever directly satisfies his wants with the produce of his own labour, creates, indeed, use-values, but not commodities (C1, p. 48; MEW, 23, p. 55).

And concerning the transformation of things with use values into commodities, Marx remarks that

> it is only by being exchanged that the products of labor acquire, as values, one uniform social status, distinct from the sensually different ways by which they can exist as objects of utility. This division of a product into a useful thing and a value becomes practically important, only when exchange has acquired such an extension that useful articles are produced for the purpose of being exchanged, and their character as values has therefore to be taken into account, beforehand, during production (MEW, 23, p. 87; translation mine).[3]

We have seen that Marx distinguishes between two forms of value which a product of labor can assume and that the capitalist who produces for the market is interested in the exchange value of a commodity. "Hence commodities must be realised as values before they can be realised as use-values," writes Marx, since the commodities will not be brought to market (that is, they will not be purchasable for use) in case they do not yield the appropriate exchange value (C1, p. 89; MEW, 23, p. 100). As the product of labor assumes a different form of value in exchange, so does the labor embodied in the product.

> At first sight, a commodity presented itself to us as a complex of two things—use-value and exchange-value. Later on, we saw also that labour, too, possesses the same two-fold nature; for, so far as it finds expression in value, it does not possess the same characteristics that belong to it as a creator of use-values (C1, pp. 48-49; MEW, 23, p. 56).

All productive activity is "nothing but the expenditure of human labour-power . . . productive expenditure of human brains, nerves, and muscles." (C1, p. 51; MEW, 23, p. 58). Although the above is the case, productive activity which produces a thing with a particular use value is qualitatively different from that which produces a different object of utility. Thus, "tailoring and weaving are necessary factors in the creation of the use-values, coat and linen, precisely because these two kinds of labour are of different qualities " (C1, p. 52). With respect to the general definition of productive activity, tailoring and weaving are only "two different modes of expending human labour-power" (C1, p. 51). Nevertheless, these two different modes of productive activity are characteristic of the production of very distinct use values such as coats and linen. If in the production and exchange of commodities exchange value is of prime importance, the mode of expending human labor power also becomes unimportant in the process of exchange. What gives a product a particular use value is the distinct skill that transforms the elements of nature into an object of utility. Thus, use value is created by a particular mode of expending labor power. Exchange value, on the other hand, is not derived from any particular mode of expending labor power. Whether a product will exchange against other goods in certain proportions is not dependent on the quality (mode) of the labor power expended, but on its quantity. Accordingly, commodity production is bound only by the quantity of "productive expenditure of human brains, nerves and muscles" and not by any mode in which human brains, nerves and muscles are expended in the process of production. The mere quantitative expenditure of human brains, nerves, and muscles, however, is an activity of which any individual is capable. It is simple labor. Since simple labor is the common denominator of all human beings, it is incapable of reflecting the uniqueness of human labor which, through its particular mode, creates a certain use value.

Exchange value, then, is not determined by any particular mode of expended labor power. According to Marx, "The value of a commodity represents human labour in the abstract, the expenditure of human labour in general" (C1, p. 51) (MEW, 23, p. 59). A commodity, he says, "may be the product of the most skilled labour, but its value, by equating it to the product of simple unskilled labour, represents a definite quantity of the latter labour alone" (C1, p. 51).[4] At another place he writes:

> On the one hand all labour is, speaking physiologically, an expenditure of human labour-power, and in its character of identical abstract human labour, it creates and forms the value of commodities. On the other hand, all labour is the expenditure of human labour-power in a special form and with a definite aim, and in this, its character of concrete useful labour, it produces use-values" (C1, p. 53; MEW, 23, p. 61).

For a commodity to be exchanged in certain proportions, it must be compared with other goods. The proportion in which a certain commodity exchanges against other commodities is determined by the quantity of abstract simple labor embodied in it. Essentially, individuals who exchange commodities merely compare the amount of simple labor embodied in each commodity and equate the labor of others on a society-wide scale:

> Whenever by an exchange, we equate as values our different products, by that very act, we also equate, as human labour, the different kinds of labour expended upon them. We are not aware of this, nevertheless we do it. Value, therefore, does not stalk about with a label describing what it is (C1, p. 79; MEW, 23, p. 88).

Although exchange is possible on this basis and although the capitalist can recover his initial outlay and augment his total capital on the basis of such exchange, a contradiction is involved. In the act of exchange, two things of different use value are equated and then exchanged in certain proportions as if their use values could be equated. Marx accepts Aristotle's view and, quoting Aristotle, claims that " 'it is . . . in reality impossible that such unlike things can be commensurable'—i.e., qualitatively equal." Nevertheless, individuals do exchange things of different use value in certain proportions as if use value could be equated and quantified. "Such an equalisation can only be something foreign to their real nature" (C1, p. 65; MEW, 23, p. 74), that is, to the real nature of the things with different use values to be exchanged. The contradiction exists insofar as commodities are exchanged for use. Use value is not quantifiable, however. Although a commodity has an exchange value that makes this commodity acquirable for use, what is measured is not the commodity's use value but the quantity of abstract labor power embodied in it.

In summary, Marx lists three peculiarities that arise when things of unequal use value are exchanged: (1) "Use-value becomes the form of manifestation, the phenomenal form of its opposite, value" (C1, p. 62; MEW, 23, p. 70); (2) "concrete labour becomes the form under which its opposite, abstract human labour, manifests itself" (C1, p. 64; MEW, 23, p.73); and (3) "the labour of private individuals takes the form of its opposite, labour directly social in its form" (C1, p. 64; MEW, 23, p. 73). The labor of private individuals can be said to become social in its form in the sense that private labor must produce use value for others (C1, p. 78; MEW, 23, p. 88). This is so because the worker is forced to produce according to an alien will and because he is prevented from appropriating his own product of labor. Instead, he must produce for a market; he must produce commodities that the capitalist will sell to the highest bidder. The worker must produce commodities which when exchanged will be of utility to others. Just because labor has become social in its form—"although, like all other commodity-producing labour, it is the labour of private individuals"— it manifests itself in products that are "directly exchangeable with other commodities" (C1, p. 64; MEW, 23, p. 73). Accordingly, Marx states in the third volume of *Capital*:

No producer, whether industrial or agricultural, when considered by himself alone, produces value or commodities. His product becomes a value and a commodity only in the context of definite social interrelations. In the first place, in so far as it appears as the expression of social labour, hence in so far as the individual producer's labour-time counts as a part of the social labour-time in general; and, secondly, this social character of his labour appears impressed upon his product through its pecuniary character and through its general exchangeability determined by its price (C3, pp. 638-639; MEW, 25, pp. 651-652).

Since, in order for commodity exchange to occur, it must reduce all qualitatively different private labor to abstract labor (the mere expenditure of human brains, nerves, and muscles), it becomes social in its nature, being based on the most common denominator underlying all labor regardless of its different qualities. However, labor is social not only in its nature, but in distinct ways. From the moment things of utility are produced for exchange,

> the labour of the individual producer acquires socially a two-fold character. On the one hand, it must, as a definite useful kind of labour, satisfy a definite social want, and thus hold its place as part and parcel of the collective labour of all, as a branch of a social division of labour that has sprung up spontaneously. On the other hand, it can satisfy the manifold wants of the individual producer himself, only in so far as the mutual exchangeability of all kinds of useful private labour is an established social fact, and therefore the private useful labour of each producer ranks on an equality with that of all others (C1, p. 78; MEW, 23, p. 87); see also MEW, 23, p. 89).[5]

Insofar as a producer can satisfy his manifold wants only by exchanging the product of his labor, he must be indifferent to the use value of the product of his labor. Exchange and exchange value become more important than use value, once commodity exchange has reached a certain scale.

> The product is increasingly produced as a commodity in the strict sense of the word, its exchange-value becomes the more independent of its immediate existence as use-value—in other words its production becomes more and more independent of its consumption by the producers and of its existence as use-value for the producers—the more one-sided it itself becomes, and the greater the variety of commodities for which it is exchanged, the greater the kinds of use-values in which its exchange-value is expressed, and the larger the market for it becomes. The more this happens, the more the product can be produced as a commodity; therefore also on an increasingly *large scale*. The producers' indifference to the use-value of his product is expressed quantitatively

in the amounts in which he produces it, which bear no relation to his own consumption needs, even when he is at the same time a consumer of his own product" (C3, pp. 268-269; MEW, 25, p. 264).

SURPLUS VALUE AND EXPLOITATION

Since all value originates in labor, the worker can be said to work for the capitalist without being compensated fully. He is forced to supply surplus labor, the product of which becomes surplus value on exchange. The capitalist as an individual is the mere personification of capital, while the worker is the mere personification of labor. The capitalist is also constrained in his behavior by competition, that is, by capital as it is personified through other capitalists. Therefore, the rate at which surplus value is extracted depends not so much on the individual capitalist as on capital as a whole and as personified by all its agents. Although the rate at which surplus value is extracted from labor may vary, capital's "single life impulse, the tendency to create value and surplus-value" (C1, p. 224) remains.[6] Hence, its emphasis is on exchange value and not on use value, since it is only through exchange that surplus value can be realized. The economy comes to a halt not because the needs that are met through use values are satisfied, but because profits that are based on exchange value are not realized (MEW, 25, p. 269):

> [C]apitalist production is in itself indifferent to the particular use-value, and distinctive features of any commodity it produces. In every sphere of production it is only concerned with producing surplus-value, and appropriating a certain quantity of unpaid labour incorporated in the product of labour. And it is likewise in the nature of the wage labour subordinated by capital that it is indifferent to the specific character of its labour and must submit to being transformed in accordance with the requirement of capital and to being transferred from one sphere of production to another (C3, p. 195; MEW, 25, p. 205).[7]

Capital's simple life impulse is the creation of value and surplus value by compelling workers to create surplus in a process of production in which labor controls neither the process of production nor the product of its own labor. In this sense, it is possible to speak of exploitation. Marx states that production founded on capital creates a situation in which man exploits man (MEW, 23, p. 743), that is, capital exploits labor (MEW, 23, p. 309). It also creates a

> system of general exploitation of the natural and human qualities, a system of general utility, utilising science itself just as much as all the physical and mental qualities, while there appears nothing *higher in itself*, nothing legitimate for itself, outside this circle of social production and exchange (G, p. 409; MEW, p. 313).

Historically, capitalist production is not the "inventor" of surplus value. Thus, if, historically speaking,

> the labourer needs all his time to produce the necessary means of subsistence for himself and his race, he has no time left in which to work gratis for others. Without a certain degree of productiveness in his labour, he has no such superfluous time at his disposal; without such superfluous time, no surplus-labour and therefore no capitalists, no slave-owners, no feudal lords, in one word no class of large proprietors (translation mine; MEW, 23, p. 534).[8]

According to Marx, capitalist production is the most effective system of exploitation.

> [E]very enterprise engaged in commodity production becomes at the same time an enterprise exploiting labour-power. But only the capitalist production of commodities has become an epoch-making mode of exploitation, which, in the course of its historical development, revolutionises, through the organisation of the labour-process and the enormous improvement of technique, the entire economic structure of society in a manner eclipsing all former epochs (C2, p. 37; MEW, 24, p. 42).

The question may be asked as to why the capitalist system is most successful in exploiting labor power, that is, in appropriating surplus labor. Marx's answer is unequivocal:

> [I]t is . . . clear that in any given economic formation of society, where not the exchange-value but the use-value of the product predominates, surplus-labour will be limited by a given set of wants which may be

greater or less, and that here no boundless thirst for surplus-labour arises from the nature of the production itself. Hence in antiquity over-work becomes horrible only when the object is to obtain exchange-value in its specific independent money-form; in the production of gold and silver (C1, p. 226; MEW, 23, p. 250).

As soon as production becomes primarily production for exchange, certain processes are set in motion which will promote particularly extreme exploitation, which according to Marx can be witnessed under capital and commodity-producing slavery. In a commodity-producing economy, the more immediate community ceases to be the primary consumer of its products. Instead, those whose exchange bid is the highest become the consumers.

Hence the negro labour in the Southern States of the American Union preserved something of a patriarchal character, so long as production was chiefly directed to immediate local consumption. But in proportion, as the export of cotton became of vital interest to these states, the over-working of the negro and sometimes the using up of his life in 7 years of labour became a factor in a calculated and calculating system. It was no longer a question of obtaining from him a certain quantity of useful products. It was now a question of production of surplus-labour itself (C1, pp. 226-227; MEW, 23, p. 250).

Under capital, high wages do not prove the absence of exploitation. The boundless thirst for surplus value exists even then.

[T]he whole capitalist system of production turns on the prolongation of this gratis labour [i.e., surplus-labour] by extending the working day or by developing the productivity, i.e., the greater intensity of labour power, etc., that, consequently, the system of wage labour is a system of slavery, and indeed a slavery which becomes more severe in proportion as the social productive forces of labour develop, whether the worker receives better or worse payment (CGP, p. 15; MEW, 19, p. 26; see also MEW, EB 1.T., p. 473).

As capitalist commodity production becomes increasingly efficient and widespread, exploitation also increases under capital, just as it did under slavery which became increasingly commodity-producing.

DISCUSSION

Marx maintains that commodity production was present in most historical periods, because at least some use value was produced for exchange and
for use by communities other than one's own. He argues that in historical
periods with commodity production such production was based on exploitation. Although he may be correct in the historical sense, it is conceivable
that commodity production could exist without exploitation, and vice
versa. Hypothetically speaking, for example, commodity production could
exist without exploitation wherever isolated producers whose labor productivity is high enough produce some of their products specifically for a
market. It could also exist in a society where the total product of labor
is collectively appropriated, providing the community as a whole also produces for exchange. On the other hand, exploitation alone could take place
even if no products are specifically produced for exchange as long as some
numbers of the society have the power to coerce others into producing
more than they need and are able to appropriate this surplus.

Engels has a comment on this topic. When Marx states that in order for
a worker to produce a commodity "he must not only produce use-values,
but use-values for others, social use-values," Engles interjects as follows:

> And not only for others, without more. The medieval peasant pro-
> duced quit-rent-corn for his feudal lord and tithe-corn for his parson.
> But neither the quit-rent-corn nor the tithe-corn became commodities
> by reason of the fact that they had been produced for others. To be-
> come a commodity a product must be transferred to another, whom it
> will serve as a use-value, by means of an exchange (C1, p. 48; MEW, 23,
> p. 55).[9]

> I am inserting the parenthesis because its omission has often given rise
> to the misunderstanding that every product that is consumed by some
> one other than its producer is considered in Marx a commodity (C1, p. 48)

It can therefore be concluded that the quit-rent-corn consumed by the
feudal lord, although the product of exploitation, is neither a commodity
nor the result of commodity production. Not all quit-rent-corn may be
consumed, however, in which case it may be exchanged for other things

and thus assume the nature of a commodity. This exchange may be accidental in the sense that only the corn left over after the lord's consumption, if any, may be exchanged. Exchange may also be planned, in which case the amount of quit-rent-corn demanded from the peasant is set at a level that will predictably allow for exchange. In this sense, the peasant, as labor under capital, is forced to produce things specifically for exchange, the difference being that the peasant's livelihood does not completely depend on the exchange of his total product. Rather, the peasant reproduces his labor for himself, while the worker under capital is prevented from doing so, so much so that even his existence comes to be threatened (TS3, p. 416; MEW, 26.3, p. 408). Only the peasant's surplus, and not his total product, is appropriated by another class. The surplus product produced may be appropriated to a greater or lesser extent, thus reflecting a higher or lower level of exploitation, or more or less commodity production. Engels' remark should not be understood to mean that, under feudalism, commodity production did not exist. It should merely indicate that not all the products of surplus labor become commodities, even though they are appropriated and consumed by individuals other than the producers.

Marx's examples suggest that for him commodity-producing slavery and the capitalist mode of production primarily lend themselves to a boundless thirst for surplus labor. While exploitation was often quite horrible under feudalism, we must conclude that Marx does not believe that there existed a boundless thirst for surplus labor under feudalism which arose directly "from the nature of the production itself."

Here it may be objected that the feudal lords were in competition for land and that, therefore, each individual feudal lord was also constrained by the actions of all the members of his class. According to Marx, the individual capitalist also does not determine the level of surplus labor extracted from the workers and the level of recklessness brought upon them. He, too, is constrained in his action by competition, that is, by capital (personfied in the capitalists) as a whole. Similarly, it may be argued that the level of exploitation in feudalism was set and determined not by the wants of any particular lord, but by the level of competition among the lords. Furthermore, since there was competition for land, theoretically, as under capital, a boundless thirst for surplus labor could develop depending on the level and nature of competition. No doubt, the burden on the peasants was often extreme. Why, then, according to Marx, did this boundless thirst not develop under feudalism? Aside from the fact that the acquisition of land did not totally depend on the level of surplus labor extracted, as is shown by feudal marriage strategies, the extraction of surplus labor itself was limited by the fact that the bulk of the population controlled the means of production needed to reproduce itself. Thus, although surplus labor in its various forms needed to be made available to the lord, the production through which the feudal population secured its own existence was not dependent on the lord, and a degree of human autonomy was preserved.

This can be said neither of slavery nor of labor under capital. Marx's analogies of wage labor with slavery illustrate this fact. Because of this autonomy, productive activity could not be subject to the will of the lords and the development of commodity production was limited. Although commodity production did occur, it was limited in scale. As a result, exploitation, according to Marx, never reached the intensity it did under capital and commodity-producing slavery. Both capital and slavery systematically destroyed the health of the producers and reduced their life expectancy.

THE INABILITY TO APPROPRIATE ONE'S
PRODUCT OF LABOR AND ITS CONSEQUENCES

Under capital, the worker, in exchange for a wage, is prevented from appropriating the product of his labor. He is forced to produce in excess of what he is being compensated, and he is engaged in commodity production rather than in the production of use values to be consumed without prior exchange. Therefore, unlike feudal production, under capital the producer's total product belongs to the capitalist and is produced not for use but for exchange. That part of the total product which results from uncompensated labor (i.e. surplus labor) for the capitalist is also exchanged, and through this exchange takes on a form desirable for the capitalist. The capitalist can augment his capital, if he does not consume the surplus value, which he will again advance in a constant form as means of production and materials and a variable form as wages. In this operation, the capitalist is subject to competition which, in turn, influences the form in which capital is put back into circulation.

The manner in which capital is advanced and put into circulation determines the conditions of production to which the workers are subject. It can readily be seen that, under capital, the worker loses all control over the state of things inasmuch as he must sell his labor in order to exist and, consequently, inasmuch as he is prevented from controlling the product of his labor. Since he does not own any means of production and must sell whatever is left to him—his labor power—he even depends on the capitalists to advance capital so that he can sell his labor power in return for a livelihood. The capital advanced in the form of wages is simply objectified labor—labor that the capitalists appropriated from the workers in the first place. The worker can therefore be said to have become dependent on the product of his own labor even for his livelihood, in addition to being dependent in terms of the conditions of production. The product of his own labor confronts him in a way that he does not control in any way, not even to the extent that he can secure his existence. The product of his own labor, owned by and mediated through the capitalist in every way, confronts him as an alien force.

In the 1844 *Manuscripts*, Marx already remarks that capital is accumulated labor, which constitutes wealth. Wealth in a society is advanced "when the capitals and the revenues of a country are growing." This is possible only because

more and more of his products are being taken away from the worker, that to an increasing extent his own labour confronts him as another man's property and that the means of his existence and his activity are increasingly concentrated in the hands of the capitalist" (CW, 3, p. 237; MEW, EB 1.T., p. 473).

The fact that the product is being taken away from the worker means "that it exists *outside him,* independently, as something alien to him, and that it becomes a power on its own confronting him. It means that the life which he has conferred on the object confronts him as something hostile and alien" (CW, 3, p. 272; MEW, EB 1.T., p. 512).[10] As more and more of the producer's product is taken away from him, the worker is increasingly confronted not only by his own labor as another man's property, but by the fact that exchange relations become ever more uncontrollable. Thus, the more numerous the products are that are being taken away from him, the more expanded commodity production, the more extended commodity production has become. As the market is continually extended,[11] "its interrelations and the conditions regulating them assume more and more the form of a natural law working independently of the producer, and become ever more uncontrollable" (C3, p. 245; MEW, 25, p. 255). Marx even goes so far as to say that, for the worker, capital "piles up dangerously over and against him." The consequences are premature death, the worker's decline to a machine, more competition, and, for some, even starvation and beggary (CW, 3, p. 238; MEW, EB 1.T., p. 474).

The observable phenomenon of capital accumulation and its consequences for those who produce the wealth being accumulated are summarized by a passage from the *Grundrisse*:

> [A]ll the progress of civilization, or in other words every increase in the powers of social production (*gesellschaftliche Produktivkräfte*), if you like, in the *productive powers of labour itself*—such as results from science, inventions, division and combination of labour, improved means of communication, creation of the world market, machinery etc.—enriches not the worker but rather *capital*; hence it only magnifies again the power dominating over labour; increases only the productive power of capital. Since capital is the antithesis of the worker, this merely increases the *objective power* standing over labour. The *transformation of labour* (as living, purposive activity) into *capital* is, *in itself,* the result of the exchange between capital and labour, in so far as it gives the capitalist the title of ownership to the product of labour (and command over the same) (G, p. 308; MEW, G, p. 215).[12]

Marx compares the fact that the laborer, through the capitalist, is controlled by his own product of labor to religion: "as in religion, man is governed by the products of his own brain, so in capitalist production, he is governed by the products of his own hand" (C1, p. 582; MEW, 23, p. 649). On the other hand, Marx observes that in bourgeois society one can misleadingly think that the individual has great freedom, while in fact the opposite is the case.

> [P]recisely the *slavery of civil society* is *in appearance* the greatest *freedom* because it is in appearance the fully developed *independence* of the individual, who considers as his *own* freedom the uncurbed movement, no longer bound by a common bond or by man, of the estranged elements of his life, such as property, industry, religion, etc., whereas actually this is his fully developed slavery and inhumanity (CW, 4, p. 116; MEW, 2, p. 123).

One manifestation of capital's domination of labor and of the workers' confrontation with the product of their labor and conditions of production as powers independent and alien to them can be seen in the development and nature of the division of labor. Thus, a particular division of labor emerges with commodity production. It can be said that

> [T]o all the different varieties of values in use there correspond as many different kinds of useful labour, classified according to the order, genus, species, and variety to which they belong in the social division of labour. This division of labour is a necessary condition for the production of commodities, but it does not follow, conversely, that the production of commodities is a necessary condition for the division of labour. In the primitive Indian community there is social division of labour, without production of commodities (C1, p. 49; MEW, 23, p. 56).

It is not only in *Capital* that Marx made this observation concerning the origin and nature of the division of labor. As was shown earlier, estrangement occurs when man must subject his will to an alien will in order to gain an existence and when, as a result, he is also prevented from appropriating the product of his own labor. The product of his own labor, capital, confronts him in its various forms as constant and variable capital. As a result, certain conditions of labor are imposed on the worker:

> *[L]abour* is only an expression of human activity within alienation, of the manifestation of life as the alienation of life, the *division of labour,* too is therefore nothing else but the *estranged, alienated* positing of human activity as a *real activity of the species* or as *activity of man as a species-being* (CW, 3, p. 317; MEW, EB 1.T., p. 557).

Estrangement from the product of one's labor, as well as the accompanying division of labor based on alienated labor, can exist only if private property exists. Without the institution of private property, the private appropriation of the products of the labor of others would be impossible, and the worker could not become dependent on the capitalist's resources for his existence. Likewise, since the division of labor under capital is expressive of "nothing else but the estranged, alienated positing of human activity," it is also dependent and rests on private property (CW, 3, p. 321; MEW, EB 1.T., p. 561).[13]

In the *Grundrisse,* Marx postulates that "exchange and division of labour reciprocally condition one another" (G, p. 158; MEW, G, p. 76). With capital's boundless thirst for surplus value, realized, in part, by increasing the volume of commodities exchanged, the division of labor increases and the increased division of labor further enhances an expansion of exchange. Marx observes that, through this process, which has a momentum of its own, the amount of simple labor in a society also increases. "Just as in bourgeois society,"[14]

> a general or a banker plays a great part, but mere man, on the other hand, a very shabby part, so here with mere human labour. It is the expenditure of simple labour-power, i.e., of the labour-power which, on an average, apart from any special development, exists in the organism of every ordinary individual. Simple average labour, it is true, varies in character in different countries and at different times, but in a particular society it is given. Skilled labour counts only as simple labour intensified, or rather, as multiplied simple labour, a given quantity of skilled being considered equal to a greater quantity of simple labour. Experience shows that this reduction is constantly being made (C1, p. 51; MEW, 23, p. 59).

An illustration from *The Poverty of Philosophy* may make this point somewhat clearer: "[W]hat characterises the division of labour inside modern society is that it engenders specialties, specialists, and with them craft-idiocy" (CW, 6, p. 190; MEW, 4, p. 157). And in *Capital* Marx writes that "not only is the detail work distributed to the different individuals, but the individual himself is made the automatic motor of a fractional operation." (C1, p. 340; MEW, p. 340).

NOTES

1. Consider the following statement in this context:

> It would be wrong to say that labour which produces use-values is the *only* source of the wealth produced by it, that is of material wealth. Since labour is an activity which adapts for some purpose or other, it needs material as a prerequisite. Different use-values contain very different proportions of labour and natural products, but use-value always comprises a natural element (CPE, p. 36; MEW, 13, p. 23).

2. It should be kept in mind that when Marx speaks of exchange value, he often merely uses the word *Wert* (value). Also, when writing exchange value rather than value only, the following passage in *Capital* is of importance:

> When at the beginning of this chapter, we said, in common parlance, that a commodity is both use-value and exchange-value, we were, accurately speaking, wrong. A commodity is a use-value or object of utility, and a value. It manifests itself as this two-fold thing, that it is, as soon as its value assumes an independent form—viz., the form of exchange value. It never assumes this form when isolated, but only when placed in a value or exchange relation with another commodity of a different kind. When once we know this, such a mode of expression does no harm; it simply serves as an abbreviation (C1, p. 66; MEW, 23, p. 75; see also Engels' comment in C1, p. 48; MEW, 23, p. 55).

3. The word *sinnlich* (sensual) remains untranslated in C1, p. 78. This is a lack inasmuch as man assesses the utility of an object through sense perception, while value is not determined through sense perception.

4. For Marx, skilled labor is labor that, through some training, requires faculties that go beyond the mere expenditure of human brains, nerves, and muscles. Since training requires an initial expenditure, skilled labor, he states, commands higher wages. It is not that its real wages are higher and that therefore the surplus product produced by it less; it is exploited to the same degree (MEW, 23, pp. 212, 360; MEW, 25, pp. 151, 311).

The above concepts must be viewed with some skepticism. As Marx writes in a footnote:

> The distinction between skilled and unskilled labour rests in part on pure illusion, or to say the least, on distinctions that have long since ceased to be real, and that survive only by virtue of a traditional convention; in part on the helpless condition of some groups of the working-class, a condition that prevents them from exacting equally with the rest the value of their labour-power. Accidental circumstances here play so great a part, that these two forms of labour sometimes change places. Where, for instance, the physique of the working class has deteriorated, and is, relatively speaking, exhausted, which is the case in all countries with a well developed capitalist production, the lower forms of labour, which demand great expenditure of muscle, are in general considered as skilled, compared with much more delicate forms of labour; the latter sink down to the level of unskilled labour (C1, p. 192; MEW, 23, p. 212).

5. For additional elaboration or commentary on social labour, see C1, pp. 78, 80; MEW, 23, pp. 88, 90; and C3, pp. 81-82, 88, 104, 516; MEW, 25, pp. 92, 99, 113, 533. Among other things, in MEW 25, Marx directly relates credit, waste of human lives, and so on to the social nature of labor, that is, that all production is commodity production.

In this context, it is useful to point out the meaning of terms such as "average simple labor," "average labor," "universal labor," "cooperative labor," "directly associated labor," and "common labor":

1. *"einfache Durchschnittsarbeit* is "simple labour power . . . which, on an average, apart from any special development, exists in the organism of every ordinary individual" (C1, p. 51; MEW, 23, p. 59 and see also p. 213).

2. *Durchschnittsarbeit* (average labor) can also mean "average paid labor" (see MEW, 25, p. 311).

3. *allgemeine Arbeit* (universal labor) and *gemeinschaftliche Arbeit* (co-operative labor):

> Both kinds play their role in the process of production, both flow one into the other, but both are also differentiated. Universal labour is all scientific labour, all discovery and all inventions. This labour depends partly on the utilisation of the labours of those who have gone before. Co-operative labour, on the other hand, is the direct co-operation of individuals (C3, p. 104; MEW, 25, p. 114).

4. Marx uses *vergesellschaftete Arbeit* inconsistently. Thus, it can mean "associated labor, or common labor" as is required, for example, to operate big machinery (C1, pp. 364-365; MEW, 23, p. 407). It can also mean "directly associated" labor as is made clear in the sentence "Owen pre-supposed directly associated labour, a form of production that is entirely inconsistent with the production of commodities" (C1, pp. 97-98; MEW, 23, pp. 109-110).

6. The capitalist does not buy labor power in order to satisfy, through the product of this labor, his personal wants or needs. He buys it for the production of surplus value (C1, p. 580; MEW, 23, p. 647).

7. Marx makes the same observation elsewhere:

> [T]he *real barrier* of capitalist production is *capital itself.* It is that capital and its self-expansion appear as the starting and the closing point, the motive and the purpose of production; that production is only production for capital and not vice versa, the means of production are not mere means for a constant expansion of the living process of the *society* of producers (C3, p. 250; MEW, 25, p. 260).

8. Translation mine insofar as I render *braucht* by "needs" instread of by "wants."

> Capital has not invented surplus-labour. Wherever a part of society possesses the monopoly of the means of production, the labourer, free or not free, must add to the working-time necessary for its own maintenance an extra working-time in order to produce the means of subsistence for the owners of the means of production, whether this proprietor be the Athenian aristocrat, Etruscan theocrat, civis Romanus, Norman baron, American slave-owner, Wallachian Boyard, modern landlord or capitalist (C1, p. 226; MEW, 23, pp. 249-250).

9. However, it would be incorrect to infer that commodity production only characterizes capitalist society. In the second volume of *Capital*, Marx mentions that commodities can be produced under various modes of production:

> No matter whether commodities are the output of production based on slavery, of peasants (Chinese, Indian ryots), of communes (Dutch East Indies), of state enterprise (such as existed in former epochs of Russian history on the basis of serfdom) or of half-savage hunting tribes, etc.—as commodities and money they come face to face with the money and commodities in which the individual capital presents itself. (C2, p. 113; MEW, 24, p. 113).

In the third volume of *Capital*, we can read:

> No matter what the basis on which products are produced, which are thrown into circulation as commodities—whether the basis of the primitive community, of slave production, of small peasant and petty bourgeois, or the capitalist basis, the character of products as commodities is not altered. . . . The extent to which products enter trade and go through the merchants' hands depends on the mode of production, and reaches its maximum in the ultimate development of capitalist production, where the product is produced solely as a commodity, and not as a direct means of subsistence (C3, p. 325; MEW, 25, p. 337).

10. In *Theories of Surplus-Value* (Vol. III), Marx again states that accumulation is "the conversion of surplus-value into capital." The unpaid labor embodied in surplus labor, which has been converted into capital, confronts the worker as

> the *totality of the objective conditions of labour*. In this form it confronts him as an alien property with the result that the capital which is antecedent to his labour, appears to be independent of it. . . . the conditions of labour confront the individual worker in an ever more gigantic form and increasingly as social forces, the chance of his taking possession of them himself as is the case in small-scale industry disappears (TS3, pp. 352-353; MEW, 26.3, pp. 344-345; see also CW, 3, p. 275 and MEW, EB 1.T., p. 515 as referred to on p. 34 of the present text).

11. For reasons which, according to Marx, are inherent in capitalism but which cannot be addressed here.

12. The following quotes may further illustrate the nature of the dominating forces controlling the worker. The worker is confronted with

> capital, as master over living labour capacity, as value endowed with its own might and will . . . "All this," says Marx, "arose from the act of exchange, in which he exchanged his living labour capacity for an amount of objectified labour, except that this objectified labour—these external conditions of his being, and the independent externality (*Ausserihmsein*) (to him) of these ob-

jective conditions—now appear as posited by himself, as *his own product,* as his own self-objectification as well as the objectification of himself as a power independent of himself, which moreover rules over him, rules over him through his own actions (G, p. 453; MEW, G, p. 357).

One manifestation of the condition that the worker is dominated by his own product in such a way that everything has an alien will and is independent of him is for Marx the worker's attitude toward that which dominates him independent of his will.

Finally, we have earlier seen that, in fact, the labourer looks at the social nature of his labour, at its combination with the labour of others for a common purpose, as he would at an alien power; the condition of realising this combination is alien property, whose dissipation would be totally indifferent to him if he were not compelled to economise with it. The situation is quite different in factories owned by the labourers themselves. (C3, p. 85; MEW, 25, pp. 95-96).

[I]f landed property became *people's property* then the whole basis of capitalist production would go, the foundation on which rests the confrontation of the worker by the conditions of labour as an independent force (TS2, p. 97; MEW, 26.2, p. 97).

13. Later, I discuss to what extent estrangement is dependent only on capital rather than on private property as such, of which capital is merely one historical form.

14. C1, p. 51, leaves out bourgeois, although it is contained in MEW, 23, p. 59.

5

Marx's Evaluation of
the Condition of Man
in Precapitalist Societies

Marx illustrated his theory of estrangement by analyzing the nature of capitalist society, and he defined human nature in order to show how capitalism prevents man from living according to his nature. Based on the analysis of production and life under capital, he was able to demonstrate the various ways in which individuals are prevented from living according to their nature and from making use of the abilities they are endowed with by nature. However, because Marx's effort was devoted primarily to obtaining a better understanding of the principles governing capitalist society, it cannot necessarily be concluded that his theory of estrangement could not also be valid in the analysis of noncapitalist social formations. Thus, it remains to be investigated whether Marx's theory of estrangement contains properties that also can apply to noncapitalist societies. Of course, since Marx does not generally talk about estrangement in noncapitalist societies, this assessment will have to be based on inference.

THE DELINEATION OF THE CAPITALIST MODE OF PRODUCTION

Since commodity production seems to be a reality in various social formations, the question arises as to what exactly distinguishes capitalist production from noncapitalist production. Marx contends that the level at which commodities are produced distinguishes the two.

The product appears as a commodity in the most varied organisms of social production. Consequently what characterises capitalist production would then be only the extent to which the product is created as an article of commerce, as a commodity, and hence the extent also to which its own constituent elements must enter again as articles of commerce, as commodities, into the economy from which it emerges.

As a matter of fact capitalist production is commodity production as the general form of production. But it is so and becomes so more and more in the course of its development only because labour itself appears here as a commodity . . . . For this reason capitalist production (and hence commodity production) does not reach its full scope until the direct agricultural producer becomes a wage-labourer (C2, pp. 119-120; MEW, 24, pp. 119-120).

Capitalist production is distinguished from the outset by two character-istic features.
First. It produces its products as commodities. The fact that it produces commodities does not differentiate it from other modes of production; but rather the fact that being a commodity is the dominant and deter-mining characteristic of its products. This implies, first and foremost, that the labourer himself comes forward merely as a seller of com-modities, and thus as a free wage-labourer, so that labour appears in general as wage-labour. . . The *second* distinctive feature of the capitalist mode of production is the production of surplus-value as the direct aim and determining motive of production. Capital produces essentially capital, and does so only to the extent that it produces surplus-value. (C3, pp. 881-882; MEW, 25, pp. 887-888).

Under capital, the nature and basis of authority are clearly distinct from those in noncapitalist production. As a consequence, although the extrac-tion of surplus value is not unique to capital, the form in which it is ex-tracted differs from that in noncapitalist production.

The authority assumed by the capitalist as the personification of capital in the direct process of production, the social function performed by him in his capacity as manager and ruler of production, is essentially different from the authority exercised on the basis of production of means of slaves, serfs, etc. (C3, p. 881; MEW, 25, p. 888).

Under capital, the worker is subject to the authority of the capitalist as a result of exchange, and not as a result of human bondage and political or theocratic domination.

> Whereas, on the basis of capitalist production, the mass of direct producers is confronted by the social character of their production in the form of strictly regulating authority and a social mechanism of the labour process organised as a complete hierarchy—this authority reaching its bearers, however, only as the personification of the conditions of labour in contrast to labour, and not as political or theocratic rulers as under earlier modes of production—among the bearers of this authority, the capitalists themselves, who confront one another only as commodity owners, there reigns complete anarchy within which the social interrelations of production assert themselves only as an overwhelming natural law in relation to individual free will (C3, p. 881; MEW, 25, p. 888; see also MEW, G, pp. 367-368).

COMMUNITIES IN WHICH PROPERTY WAS HELD IN COMMON

If capitalist society is characterized by primarily commodity production, earlier noncapitalist social formations are characterized by the absence of systematic commodity production. The question arises as to what types of exchange exist in societies "based on property in common"— societies of the form of "a patriarchal family, an ancient Indian community, or a Peruvian Inca State." First, however, it must be noted that Marx distinguishes between various types of exchange. For example, he states that savages often do not exchange one particular use value for another; instead, "a chaotic mass of articles are offered as the equivalent of a single article" (C1, p. 91; MEW, 23, p. 102). Barter differs from the type of exchange often found with savages as well as from the type of exchange characteristic in capitalist society.

> The direct barter of products attains the elementary form of the relative expression of value in one respect, but not in another. That form is x Commodity A = y Commodity B. The form of direct barter is x use-value A = y use-value B. The articles A and B in this case are not as yet commodities, but become so only by the act of barter. The first step made by an object of utility towards acquiring exchange-

value is when it forms a non-use-value for its owner, and that happens
when it forms a superfluous portion of some article required for his
immediate wants (C1, p. 91; MEW, 23, p. 102).

Capitalism systematically produces more commodities than the producer
needs and, more importantly, it produces directly for exchange. Unlike a
barter economy under which products become commodities only through
the act of exchange, under capital products immediately become commodities.

In the direct barter of products, each commodity is directly a means
of exchange to its owner, and to all other persons an equivalent, but
that only insofar as it has use-value for them. At this stage, therefore,
the articles exchanged do not acquire a value-form independent of their
own use-value, or of the individual needs of the exchangers (C1, pp. 91-
92; MEW, 23, p. 103).

If, however, individuals consistently barter, exchange becomes a regular
social process and the desire for foreign use values becomes an every day
phenomenon.

[I]n the course of time, therefore, some portion at least of the products
of labour must be produced with a special view to exchange. From
that moment the distinction becomes firmly established between the
utility of an object for the purpose of consumption, and its utility
for the purposes of exchange. Its use-value becomes distinguished
from its exchange-value. On the other hand, the quantitative proportion in which the articles are exchangeable, becomes dependent on
their production itself. Custom stamps them as values with definite
magnitudes" (C1, p. 91; MEW, 23, p. 103).

Marx postulates that exchange begins at the point where the community
stops (MEW, 23, pp. 25, 102-103, 187). That is, it exists between communities. If members of two different communities engage regularly in
direct barter, their products become commodities on a regular basis, although they may not be commodities from the very outset of their production. However, "as soon . . . as products once become commodities in
the external relations of a community, they also, by reaction, become so

in its internal intercourse." The communities based on common property to which Marx referred had not yet become subject to this process. In their internal relations, products had not become commodities because the communities' external relations consisted of an exchange that at best was infrequent and erratic. While no set pattern had emerged, some exchange may have occasionally occurred.

> [T]hose small and extremely ancient Indian communities, some of which have continued down to this day, are based on possession in common of the land, on the blending of agriculture and handicrafts, and on an unalterable division of labour, which serves, whenever a new community is started, as a plan and scheme ready cut and dried. . . . The chief part of the products is destined for direct use by the community itself, and does not take the form of a commodity. Hence, production here is independent of that division of labour brought about, in Indian society as a whole, by means of the exchange of commodities. It is the surplus alone that becomes a commodity, and a portion of even that, not until it has reached the hands of the State, into whose hands from time immemorial a certain quantity of these products has found its way in the shape of rent in kind. (C1, p. 337; MEW, 23, p. 378).

It is now possible to return to our original question as to what type of exchange exists with societies "based on property in common." According to Marx, commodity production does not exist within such communities, and there is no or only minimal barter between the members. This does not mean that some individuals do not produce more than they need for themselves. On the contrary, there are surplus products, some of which are exchanged with other communities (barter), some given as tribute to government, and the rest distributed among the members. Strictly speaking, this distribution of products internal to the community "based on property in common" is a form of exchange, since the surplus of "A" may benefit "B" and inverse, or the products of one type of manufacture may benefit those who manufacture a different product (MEW, 23, pp. 378-379). The decisive point is that this process occurs without the products becoming commodities, either by being exchanged in barter fashion or, worse, by being produced for a market in which exchange value and use value have already become distinguished as separate forms of value. According to which criteria, then, are products exchanged in communities "based on property in common?" To my knowledge, Marx does not answer this question. Engels, however, says in *Anti Dühring* that both work and products for consumption are distributed according to tradition and needs (MEW, 20, p. 288). Implicitly, Marx makes the same assertion when discussing the Inca Indians: "[T]ransportation played a prominent role in the land of the Incas, although the social product neither circulated as a commodity nor was distributed by means of barter" (C2, p. 152; MEW, 24, p. 152).

COMMUNISTIC SOCIETIES BASED ON THE GENTILE ORGANIZATION

It is useful to know how Marx views societies that have no products to be exchanged or that do not exchange with other communities. As is well known, both in his views and his techniques of reasoning Marx relies heavily on the work of L. H. Morgan. Morgan's method is one of evolutionary prediction in reverse. Instead of predicting the state into which a given society will evolve, a state about which we have no information whatsoever, knowledge about the history of societies is used to infer the type of society from which they evolved. For example, information on tribal societies is used to infer the social organization from which these tribal societies evolved. Thus, the attempt is made to construct a view of society and its organizational structure for a period in human history for which we have no living examples.

In this context, it is not important to assess whether the method used by Marx, as well as Engels and Morgan, is appropriate. Nor is it imperative to discuss whether Marx was correct in his inferences concerning the original condition of societies. What is important is to note some of his views on this subject, since they will be helpful in assessing his theory of estrangement.

Unfortunately, Marx's thinking on societies in the original condition is available only in a rather incomplete and sketchy form. Through Lawrence Krader, however, some of Marx's views in the *Ethnological Notebooks* have become available to a larger circle. Largely with the help of the *Notebooks,* an attempt is made here to extract those Marxian views that may have a bearing on the interpretation of his theory of estrangement. Even so, the *Notebooks* do not give us a complete account of his thinking on societies in the original state. To escape this limitation, some use of Engels' writings will be made on this subject. Certainly it would be better to have Marx's complete views, but under the circumstances, it is better to "supplement" Marx's thinking on the subject rather than rely solely on the *Ethnological Notebooks*. This procedure is justified (1) because Engels had access to Marx's notes on Morgan and used them for his book on the origin of the family, and (2) because in view of their intimate friendship and their mutual cooperation until Marx's death, Engels' views can be assumed not to have deviated significantly from those of Marx in this respect. As Engels tells us in his foreword, Marx intended to write a book on the family similar to the one Engels wrote shortly after Marx's death in 1883. A close exchange of ideas must have taken place, and there is no evidence that the two disagreed significantly concerning communist societies based on the gentile organization.

According to Engels (MEW, 21, p. 71), Marx often said that the key to understanding our own primitive age can be found among the American Indians. This primitive age at first consisted of life in the form of hordes, a form of human life that Marx thought could not be found anymore and that was "far below the lowest savage now living" (EN, p. 125). Sexual relations at this level are characterized as *"promiscuous intercourse"* and "the *ruder flint implements* found over part of the earth's surface, and not used by existing savages, attest extreme rudeness of man's condition" (EN, p. 125). After man emerged from this primitive habitat, he commenced as a fisherman to spread over continental areas (EN, p. 125). Thus, the first stage of the family was formed. It was the consanguine family which *"recognized promiscuity within defined limits"* (EN, p. 125). Further organization into gentes (kinship) occurred within which brothers and sisters were prohibited from marrying, although monogamy had not been established and sexual access was not limited to one partner. Gens, the general name for organizational forms in which kinship was derived from one ancestral mother—since as a result of promiscuity the father was not known—were democratically organized. The council of the gens with the Iroquois was the instrument of government and had supreme authority over gens.

[E]very adult male and female member had a voice upon all questions brought before it; it *elected and deposed* its *sachem* and chiefs . . . it *condoned* or *avenged* the murder of a gentilis, it *adopted* persons into the *gens*. It was *the germ of the higher council of the tribe, and of that still higher of the confederacy, each of which was composed exclusively of chiefs as representatives of the gentes.* . . . All the members of an

Iroquois gens *personally free,* bound *to defend each other's freedom; equal in privileges and personal rights.* Sachem and chiefs claiming to superiority; a *brotherhood bound together by the ties of kin. Liberty, Equality, and Fraternity,* though never formulated, were *cardinal principles der gens* and those the *unit of a social and governmental system,* the foundation on which Indian society organized   (EN, p. 150; translation mine where necessary; see also EN, p. 162).

Marx notes that "[i]n this *lower and middle ethnical period democratic principles were the vital* element of gentile society" (EN, p. 172; translation mine where necessary). The sachems, who were the counselors of the people, were required to make unanimous decisions concerning all public questions. Such unanimity was essential to the validity of every public act (EN, p. 170; see also EN, pp. 165-166 and MEW, 21, p. 21).
    Marx also notes that all the members of an Iroquois gens were personally free. Thus, even

> *[M]ilitary questions* usually left to the *action of the voluntary principle.* Theoretically *each tribe at war with every other tribe* with which it had not formed *a treaty of peace.* Any person *at liberty to organize a war party* and conduct an expedition wohin he wollte. He *announced his project by giving a war-dance and inviting volunteers . . . When a tribe was menaced with an attack,* war parties were formed to meet it in much the same manner. Where forces so raised were united in one body, *each under its own war-captain* and *their joint movements* determined *by a council of these captains* (EN, p. 162).

Since the Iroquois were organized according to the principle of consanguinity, it can be inferred that they practiced a communistic life-style. Marx remarks that *"communism in living* seems to have originated *in the necessities of the consanguine family"* (EN, p. 115). Although a certain office may have passed from father to son, it does not follow that there was hereditary succession. As shown above, the Iroquois members of the gens had the power to elect and recall their representatives. If succession from father to son occurred, it was *"by the free consent of the people."* According to Marx, hereditary succession came *"from force* (usurpation)" (EN, p. 173).
    On this level of social and economic development, with regard to the labor time required for individuals to insure subsistence propagation of

the species, Marx comments in the *Grundrisse* that "[in] the lowest stages of production . . . few human needs have yet been produced, and thus few to be satisfied. Necessary labour is therefore restricted, not because labour is productive, but because it is not very necessary" (G, p. 398; MEW, G, p. 302). Although few products are being produced at this level of development, it does not follow that there is no surplus. However, "in the less productive stages of exchange, people exchange nothing more than their *superfluous labour time*; this is the measure of their exchange, which therefore extends only to superfluous products," while under capital "the existence of *necessary* labour time is conditional on the creation of *superfluous* labour time" (G, p. 398; MEW, G, pp. 301-302).

Certainly, Morgan's description of communism associated with consanguineous kinship relations appealed to Marx in many ways. Yet, it would be wrong to conclude that Marx "approved" of life at this stage of development and proclaimed it to be the ideal human condition. Already in the *Manuscripts,* he shows a certain kind of contempt for the "simplicity of the *poor* and crude man who has few needs and who has not only failed to go beyond private property, but has not yet even reached it" (CW, 3, p. 295; MEW, EB 1.T., p. 535). He states his objections to primitive communism more precisely in *Capital*:

[T]hose ancient social organisms of production are, as compared with bourgeois society, extremely simple and transparent. But they are founded either on the immature development of man individually, who has not yet severed the umbilical cord that unites him with his fellowmen in a primitive tribal community, or upon direct relations of subjection. They can arise and exist only when the development of the productive power of labour has not risen beyond a low stage, and when, therefore, the social relations within the sphere of material life, between man and man, and between man and nature, are correspondingly narrow (C1, pp. 83-84; MEW, 23, pp. 93-94).

In *The Origin of the Family, Private Property and the State,* Engels elaborates on this theme.

[T]he gentile constitution in its best days, as we saw it in America, presupposed an extremely sparse population over a wide area. Man's attitude to nature was therefore one of almost complete subjection to a strange incomprehensible power, as is reflected in his childish religious conceptions. Man was bounded by his tribe, both in relation to strangers from outside the tribe and to himself; the tribe, the gens, and their institutions were sacred and inviolable, a higher power established by nature, to which the individual subjected himself unconditionally in feeling, thought, and action. However impressive the people of this epoch appear to us, they are completely undifferentiated from one another; as Marx says, they are still attached to the navel string of the primitive community (OF, p. 88; MEW, 21, p. 97).

For Marx, the communistic primitive community is not the ideal state of existence, although in some respects it was attractive to him. If, at one time, these primitive societies were communistic, however, what factors contributed to the decay of this communism? In the following pages, again with the help of Engels' writings, an attempt is made to reconstruct Marx's thought concerning the historical developments that led to the "fall from the simple moral greatness of the old gentile society" (OF, p. 88) and started the process of civilization for these societies.

Engels comments that the organization of the Iroquois people was doomed to collapse and that the highest form of their social organization—the confederacy of tribes—already marked the beginning of its collapse. As evidence, he cites the Iroquois' attempts to subjugate others and the fact that war was common and only later mitigated by self-interest (OF, p. 87; MEW, 21, p. 97). The more profound source of decay lay elsewhere, however. According to Marx, the differences in the distribution of personal property were primarily responsible for the beginning crack in the foundations of communism. Marx's examples are not necessarily drawn from the Iroquois, however, since Marx's assumption is that the slightly more developed social forms from which the examples are often drawn were at one time also communistic. Consequently, evidence of the emergence of personal property is not confined to the Iroquois, and according to Marx and Engels, can also be found in the history of other societies. In the *German Ideology,* Marx and Engels propose the idea that "real private property began with the ancients, as with modern nations, with movable property" (CW, 5, p. 89; MEW, 3, p. 61). And in his *Ethnological Notebooks* Marx notes that at the stage only slightly higher in development than that of the Iroquois there is a

> *great increase in personal property* and *some changes in the relations of persons to land.* The *territorial domain still belonged to the tribe in common;* but *a portion* now set apart for *support of the govern-*

ment, another for *religious uses,* and a still *more important portion— that from which the people drew its subsistence, divided among the several gentes, or communities of persons who resided in the same pueblo.* . . . . *Individual ownership of houses and lands excluded by communal property of lands by gentes* or *communities of persons, joint-tenement houses* and *mode of occupation by related families* . . . . *Their land is held in common,* but after a person cultivates a lot he has the *personal claim to it which he can sell to one of the community.* (EN, p. 132; translation mine where necessary).

Here Marx is referring to the Laguna Pueblo Indians whom he states are an example of the stage of development slightly higher than the one of the Iroquois.

Of the Mogui Village Indians, he remarks that they "now have *flocks of sheep, horses and mules* and considerable other *personal property"* (EN, p. 132; translation mine where necessary). On this level, Engels points out that, in contrast to the lowest levels of development, a steady surplus may be produced, facilitating a regular exchange and a division of labor that is not based merely on sex, age, and physical strength (OF, p. 150; MEW, 21, p. 160).[1] Citing Marx, Engels maintains that "the property differences within one and the same gens . . . transformed its unity of interest into, antagonism between its members." These property differences were also accompanied by "greed for riches" (see also EN, p. 128) and transformed the whole gentile constitution, with its roots in the people, in gens, phratry, and tribe, into its opposite:

[F]rom an organization of tribes for the free ordering of their own affairs it becomes an organization for the plundering and oppression of their neighbors; and correspondingly its organs change from instruments of the will of the people into independent organs for the domination and oppression of the people (OF, p. 150; MEW, 21, p. 160).

According to Engels, at this point in history the threshold of civilization was reached (OF, p. 150).[2]

MARX'S USE OF THE TERM "PRIVATE PROPERTY"

In his *Ethnological Notebooks,* Marx does not, to my knowledge, use the term "private property." As we have seen, however, he does use the terms "property" (*Eigentum*), "objects of ownership" (EN, pp. 127-128), "personal property," and "individual ownership" (EN, p. 132). These terms are used in the context of describing how the original communism was undermined by the unequal accumulation of products by individuals. These may not have been isolated individuals, but in contrast to the previous form of communistic ownership, it was *personal* property and a form of private property. This may also have been Engels' reason for occasionally substituting the term *Privateigentum* (private property) with *Sondereigentum* (separate ownership of) for his later editions of *The Origin of the Family, Private Property and the State* (see MEW, 21, pp. 58, 156), while in his first edition he used *Privateigentum* with no qualification. The substitution allowed him to emphasize that it was not *Privateigentum* in the sense known today, but neither was it communal property anymore. The following passage from Engels illustrates this point:

> But to whom did this new wealth belong? Originally to the gens, without a doubt. Private property in herds must have already started at an early period, however. . . . What is certain is that we must not think of him as a property owner in the modern sense of the word. And it is also certain that at the threshold of authentic history we already find the herds everywhere separately owned (Sondereigentum) by heads of families, as are the artistic products of barbarism—metal implements, luxury articles and, finally, the human cattle—the slaves (OF, p. 48; MEW, 21, p. 58).

For Marx the term *Privateigentum* seems to refer primarily to property as appropriated in the city-states of Rome and Greece, under feudalism, and under capitalism. This can be said despite the fact that Marx, in the *German Ideology,* says that "real private property began with the ancients, as with modern nations, with movable property" (CW, 5, p. 89; MEW, 3, p. 61). On the contrary, his emphasis on real private property can be seen as a conscious distinction from the way he commonly uses the term "private property," namely, to designate the ownership of the means of production, be it in the form of feudal landholdings or machinery under capital. Thus, in the *Manuscripts,* Marx maintains that feudal property in land was the beginning of the domination of private property and that it was the root of private property (MEW, EB 1.T., pp. 505-506). In the *Manuscripts* he also states that

only at the culmination of the development of private property does
this, its secret, appear again, namely, that on the one hand it is the
product of alienated labour, and that on the other it is the *means*
by which labour alienates itself, the *realisation of this alienation*
(CW, 3, p. 280; MEW, EB 1.T., p. 520).

As a result of the private ownership of the means of production, it is possible to coerce others into giving up their product of work, or a portion
of it, in return for a wage. This, in turn, perpetuates the ability of some
to compel others to sell their labor. The owners of the means of production are able to maintain their property and accumulate more only if
surplus labor can be extracted from others, whose existence depends
on earning a wage.

The term "private property" is also used in Marx's *Theories of Surplus-
Value* in such a way as to designate clearly the private ownership of the
means of production.

The original unity between the worker and the conditions of production (abstracting from slavery, where the labourer himself belongs to
the objective conditions of production) has two main forms: the
Asiatic communal system (primitive communism) and a small-scale
agriculture based on the family (and linked with domestic industry)
in one form or another. Both are embryonic forms and both are
equally unfitted to develop labour as *social* labour and the productive
power of social labour. Hence the necessity for the separation, for
the rupture, for the antithesis of labour and property (by which
property in the conditions of production is to be understood). The
most extreme form of this rupture, and the one in which the productive forces of social labour are also most powerfully developed,
is capital. The original unity can be re-established only on the material
foundation which capital creates and by means of the revolutions
which, in the process of this creation, the working class and the whole
society undergo (TS, 3, pp. 422-423; MEW, 26.3, pp. 414-415).

And in *Capital,* Marx mentions that the "legal view of free private ownership of land, arises in the ancient world only with the dissolution of the
organic order of society, and in the modern world only with the development of capitalistic production" (C3, p. 616; MEW, 25, p. 629).

In summary, Marx reserved the term "private property" to designate private ownership of the means of production, and he used other terms to designate the privately accumulated products which were not means of production. Thus, the personal and unequal accumulation of herds and other objects which undermined the communism of the gens cannot be considered to be means of production. Accordingly, he used the term "personal property" rather than "private property." Unfortunately, Marx's death prevented him from showing how unequally accumulated personal property led to the ownership of the means of production (private property). Hence, Engels' work on the origin of the family and private property assumes an important place in the interpretation of Marx's thought.

NOTES

1. Similarly, Marx writes about the Russian community that owned large parts of land in common and combined work in agriculture with handicraft. Those communities were not engaged in commodity production and adjusted their craft activities to the agricultural seasonal production schedule. Craftmanship complemented agricultural production (MEW, 24, pp. 243-244). Thus the Russian community, too, was quite resistant to being torn apart by commerce. In this context Marx says that

> The obstacles presented by the internal solidity and organisation of pre-capitalistic, national modes of production to the corrosive influence of commerce are strikingly illustrated in the intercourse of the English with India and China. The broad basis of the mode of production here is formed by the unity of small-scale agriculture and home industry, to which in India we should add the form of village communities built upon the common ownership of land, which identically, was the original form in China as well. In India the English lost no time in exercising their direct political and economic power, as rulers and landlords, to disrupt these small economic communities. English commerce exerted a revolutionary influence on these communities and tore them apart only in so far as the low prices of its goods served to destroy the spinning and weaving industries, which were an ancient integrating element of this unity of industrial and agricultural production. And even so this work of dissolution proceeds very gradually. And still more slowly in China, where it is not reinforced by direct political power. The substantial economy and saving in time afforded by the association of agriculture with manufacture put up a stubborn resistance to the products of the big industries, whose prices include the *faux frais* of the circulation process which pervades them. Unlike the English, Russian commerce, on the other hand, leaves the economic groundwork of Asiatic production untouched (C3, pp. 333-334; MEW, 25, p. 346. See also C1, p. 333; MEW, 23, p. 372).

2. It would, of course, be incorrect to assume that the increase in personal property emerged from one day to the next. Marx notes that "the *objects of ownership* increase, of course, in every 'successive ethnical period'. . . . The growth of property is thus closely connected with the increase of inventions *and discoveries,* and the *improvements of social institutions* which mark the several ethnical periods of human progress" (EN, p. 127; translation mine where necessary). Nevertheless, a significant unequal accumulation of personal property occurred primarily at the stage of "barbarism," to use Morgan's terminology, which was adopted by Marx and Engels. Concerning the decay of the Greek gens, Engels shows how changes in inheritance patterns led to unequal accumulation on the part of individuals. The fact that specific individuals of a household rather than the community of gentiles inherited the possessions of individuals after the death of individuals (see EN, p. 128) was crucial for the future of communism based on gens. Engels writes:

> Thus in the Greek constitution of the heroic age we see the old gentile order as still a living force. But we also see the beginnings of its disintegration: father-right, with transmission of the property to the children, by which accumulation of wealth within the family was favored and the family itself became a power as against the gens; reaction of the inequality of wealth on the constitution by the formation of the first rudiments of hereditary nobility and monarchy; slavery, at first only of prisoners of war, but already preparing the way for the enslavement of fellow-members of the tribe and even of the gens; the old wars between tribe and tribe already degenerating into systematic pillage by land and sea for the acquisition of cattle, slaves and treasure, and becoming a regular source of wealth; in short, riches praised and respected as the highest good and the old gentile order misused to justify the violent seizure of riches (OF, pp. 96-97; MEW, 21, p. 105).

Similarly, Engels comments at the end of his chapter on the Iroquois:

> [T]he power of this primitive community had to be broken, and it was broken. But it was broken by influences which from the very start appear as a degradation, a fall from the simple moral greatness of the old gentile society. The lowest interests—base greed, brutal appetites, sordid avarice, selfish robbery of the common wealth—inaugurate the new, civilised, class society. It is by the vilest means—theft, violence, fraud, treason—that the old classless gentile society is undermined and overthrown (OF, p. 88; MEW, 21, p. 97).

Krader suggests that "in Marx's conception the office of the chief had been opposed to the collectivity within it not only in the period of the dissolution of the gens and tribe, but before, since, contrary to Morgan, the chief was elected only in theory" (EN, pp. 37, 42). Krader cites Marx's excerpts on Maine as evidence:

> [T]o Maine, . . . the *quite natural function of the chief of the gens, furthermore of tribe,* natural just because he is their *chief* (and theoretically always "elected"),

appears as "artificial" and "mere administrative authority," whereby, from the archaic point of view, it is exactly the arbitrariness of the modern *pater familias,* as the private family, which is "artificial" (EN, p. 309; translation mine where necessary).

Marx's remark "theoretically always 'elected' " does not warrant the conclusion that the chief was "elected *only* (my emphasis) in theory" and that Marx perceived the office of the chief to be in opposition to the collectivity. To be certain about this, one would need additional information, but such evidence was not found in Engels or Marx, nor does Krader cite additional evidence. Moreover, in the quoted excerpt on Maine, Marx does not seem to directly evaluate whether the office of the chief was in opposition to the collectivity. He merely states that theoretically the chief was always elected. However, he indirectly evaluates the extent to which the chief's position was not arbitrary when he asserts that the position of the modern paterfamilias was artificial. Marx seems to make the point, against Maine, that, since the chief is in theory always elected, his position, contrary to that of the paterfamilias, was not arbitrary and artificial. If anything can be concluded, it would be the opposite of what Krader concluded, namely, that the office of the chief was not necessarily in opposition to the collectivity.

Krader may also put a somewhat misplaced emphasis on Marx's thinking on right and obligation:

> Hegel had conceived the political relation as the balance of right and obliga-
> tion; in this matter, Marx had followed him. . . . In the community the balance
> of right and obligation is a traditional development, whereas in the polity
> the balance must be redeveloped by appeal to force, to reason, to sentiment
> on disposition, and the like; in the latter case the balance becomes artificial,
> as a device of civilization (EN, p. 67).

However, Engels writes that for the community, that is, the gentile communistic organization before it reached the threshold of civilization, the distinction between rights and duties cannot be made.

> This simple organization suffices completely for the social conditions out of
> which it sprang. It is nothing more than the grouping natural to those condi-
> tions, and it is capable of settling all conflicts that can arise within a society
> so organized. War settles external conflicts; it may end with the annihilation
> of the tribe, but never with its subjugation. It is the greatness, but also the
> limitation, of the gentile constitution that it has no place for ruler and ruled.
> Within the tribe there is as yet no difference between rights and duties; the
> question whether participation in public affairs, in blood revenge or atone-
> ment, is a right or a duty, does not exist for the Indian; it would seem to him
> just as absurd as the question whether it was a right or a duty to sleep, eat,
> or hunt (OF, p. 144; MEW, 21, pp. 132-133).

The question, then, is not one of a balance of right and obligation as Krader, without citing Marx, suggests. Rather, it is one of the existence or nonexistence of the notions of right and obligation. If, in the absence of other evidence, we can take Engels' view as a proper reflection of what Marx thinks on this topic, it must be concluded that Marx did not think of life in the gentile communistic organization as one in which rights and obligations are balanced, be it through traditional development or not. One would have to perceive of life in such a society as subject to no other means of social control than public opinion, and also outside the realm of *any* definition of what is right and what is obligation. Hence, the question of balance between right and obligation would not even enter into the picture. It is Engels' view that public opinion was the only means of coercion. For him, "the gentile organization had grown out of a society which knew no internal contradictions, and it was only adapted to such a society. It possessed no means of coercion except public opinion" (OF, p. 154; MEW, 21, p. 164).

6

The Division of Labor and Its Centrality for Marx's Theory of Estrangement

According to Marx, the division of labor under the communism of primitive society was based on age, sex, and physical strength (MEW, 23, p. 372). This division was, therefore, not yet a true division of labor. "Division of labour only becomes truly such from the moment when a division of material and mental labour appears" (CW, 5, pp. 44-45; MEW, 3, p. 31). At this point, however, private property has also arisen. "Division of labour and private property are, after all, identical expressions: in the one the same thing is affirmed with reference to activity as is affirmed in the other with reference to the product of the activity" (CW, 5, p. 46; MEW, 3, p. 32).

Marx's treatment of the emergence of the division of labor is similar to that of the emergence of private property. Although there was personal property at earlier stages of development, it was not private property as Marx tends to use the term; and although there had been a division of labor, it became truly one only with the emergence of private property— with the emergence of a division between mental and material labor. In *Capital*, Marx also postulates that true division of labor goes beyond a physiologically based one and is accompanied by exchange. It is based on exchange and on the trend that products have become commodities

(MEW, 23, pp. 372-373). Thus private property, commodity exchange, and a society-wide division of labor that is not based on physiology occur simultaneously, at least for analytical purposes, in the *Ethnological Notebooks;* however Marx very well realizes that there may be some "grey areas."

The division of labor occurs on two different levels: on the level of a society as a whole, and on the level of a firm, for example, among individual workers. In precapitalist society, the division of labor on the level of the whole society emerged from the "material conditions of production" and was legally formalized much later. Marx believes that this was the case under patriarchal regimes as well as under the feudal and caste systems. Under these forms of social organization, the division of labor of the whole society was based on distinct rules of authority, while in capitalist society there is no such distinct rule (MEW, 4, p. 151): "[M]odern society knows no other rule, no other authority for the distribution of labor than free competition" (MEW, 4, p. 151; translation mine).[1] Marx postulates that since, on the level of society, the only other authority that determines the division of labor is free competition, the more the division of labor is determined by the entrepreneur's authority on the level of the firm. As long as the societal division of labor was based on legally formalized rules, the division of labor in the various production shops was little developed (MEW, 4, p. 151). The following rule can be established:

> The less the division of labor within a society is determined by an authority, the more is the division of labor developed within a workshop and the more it is subject to the authority of a single individual. Accordingly, with respect to the division of labor, the authority in the workshop and the one in the society are in an inverse relationship to each other (MEW, 4, p. 151; translation mine;[2] see also MEW, 23, p. 378 and C1, p. 337 where Marx reiterates this idea).

At this point Marx compares the division of labor under capitalist and precapitalist societies.

> If, in a society with capitalist production, anarchy in the social division of labour and despotism in that of the workshop are mutual conditions the one of the other, we find, on the contrary, in those earlier forms of

society in which the separation of trades has been spontaneously developed, then crystallized, and finally made permanent by law, on the
one hand, a specimen of the organisation of the labour of society, in
accordance with an approved and authoritative plan, and on the other,
the entire exclusion of division of labour in the workshop, or at all
events a mere dwarflike or sporadic and accidental development of
the same (C1, p. 337; MEW, 23, pp. 377-378).

The division of labor on the shop level is enhanced by the fact that the
workers in a particular workshop become more numerous (MEW, 4, p. 152),
and by the increased concentration of the means of production and the
introduction of machinery that tended to accompany this concentration
(MEW, 4, p. 153; see also MEW, EB 1.T., p. 473). Marx suggests that, on
the whole, machinery increased the division of labor in society, simplified
work in the shop, concentrated capital, and fractionalized man (CW, 6,
p. 188; MEW, 4, p. 155). Since the division of labor increases with the
concentration of the tools of production, he proposes that each significant
invention in mechanical technique results in an increased division of labor.
In itself, this division calls for new mechanical inventions (MEW, 4, p. 154),
producing a trend toward ever simpler, unskilled labor (MEW, 13, p. 18).
Although the worker as a worker loses in general productive ability because
his level of skill falls, the productive power of capital increases. "The division of labour develops the *social* productive power of *social* labour, but
at the expense of the *general productive ability* of the worker" (TS2, p. 234;
MEW, 26.2, p. 232). In this respect, Marx follows Adam Smith who held
that "the farmer practices a trade requiring more intelligence than the manu-
facturing worker, who is subject to the division of labour" (TS2, p. 234).
The increased social productive power—brought about by an increase in
the division of labor—however, "confronts the worker . . . as an increased
productive power, *not of his* labour, but of *capital,* the force that dominates
his labour" (TS2, p. 234).

The capitalist mode of production is not the only case in which an increase in the division of labor can be said to have consequences that are
beyond the control of individuals and that can affect their lives in ways
not necessarily expected originally. An economy with trade relations exceed-
ing those of a barter economy, but not reaching the magnitude of capitalist exchange relations, may be taken as an example.

[T]he circulation of commodities differs from the direct exchange of products (barter), not only in form, but in substance . . . B's commodity replaces that of A, but A and B do not mutually exchange those commodities. It may, of course, happen that A and B make simultaneous purchases, the one from the other; but such exceptional transactions are by no means the necessary result of the general conditions of the circulation of commodities. We see here, on the one hand, how the exchange of commodities breaks through all local and personal bounds inseparable from direct barter, and develops the circulation of the products of social labour; and on the other hand, now it develops a whole network of social relations spontaneous in their growth and entirely beyond the control of the actors (C1, pp. 113-114; MEW, 23, p. 126; see also MEW, 23, p. 121).

Although the barter-type of exchange differs in form and substance from an economy involving a currency, still Marx believes that an established barter economy tends to enhance commodity production. The enhancement of commodity production, however, is likely to lead to forms of exchange involving a currency and enhancing the further division of labor on the basis that a greater number of transactions can take place in or between given societies. Therefore,

circulation bursts through all restrictions as to time, place, and individuals, imposed by direct barter, and this it effects by splitting up, into the antithesis of a sale and a purchase, the direct identity that in barter does exist between the alienation of one's own and the acquisition of some other man's product (C1, p. 115; MEW, 23, p. 127).

Since circulation bursts through all restrictions as to time, place, and individuals, Marx concludes that the division of labor in manufacture, for example, excluding modern industry based on machinery,

acquires the best adapted form at first by experience, as it were behind the backs of the actors, and then, like the guild handicrafts, strives to hold fast that form when once found, and here and there succeeds in keeping it for centuries. Any alteration in this form, except in trivial matters, is solely owing to a revolution in the instruments of labour (C1, p. 343; MEW, 23, p. 385).

Under capital, the division of labor is determined by free competition, which itself is the result of a further increase in the number of exchange relationships. With free competition as the sole "authority . . . determining the division of labor"—and thus replacing any former authority determining the division of labor—it becomes easy to see why Marx names this state of affairs "anarchy in the social division of labor."

Marx describes how the development of commodity production proceeds until it becomes the general form of production:

> [T]he same conditions which give rise to the basic condition of capitalist production, the existence of a class of wage-workers, facilitate the transition of all commodity production to capitalist commodity production. As capitalist production develops, it has a disintegrating, resolvent effect on all older forms of production, which, designed mostly to meet the direct needs of the producer, transform only the excess produced into commodities. Captailist production makes the sale of products the main interest, at first apparently without affecting the mode of production itself. Such was for instance the first effect of capitalist world commerce on such nations as the Chinese, Indians, Arabs, etc. But, secondly, wherever it takes root capitalist production destroys all forms of commodity production which are based either on the self-employment of the producers, or merely on the sale of the excess product as commodities. Capitalist production first makes the production of commodities general and then, by degrees, transforms all commodity production into capitalist commodity production (C2, p. 36; MEW, 24, pp. 41-42).

Once commodity production becomes capitalist commodity production, the division of labor is totally uprooted from the traditionally set patterns and develops in a thoroughly unchecked manner:

> When production by means of wage-labour becomes universal, commodity production is bound to be the general form of production. This mode of production, once it is assumed to be general, carries in its wake an ever increasing division of social labour, that is to say an ever growing differentiation of the articles which are produced in the form of commodities by a definite capitalist, ever greater division of complementary process of production into independent processes (C2, pp. 35-36; MEW, 24, p. 41).

INVOLUNTARY DIVISION OF LABOR

Although the division of labor in precapitalist societies that exchanged commodities rested upon a formal authority, and was therefore not subject to the anarchic conditions created by free competition, it cannot be said that it was not based on coercion. This division of labor as well as that under capital is an involuntary division.

The division of labor and private property are two sides of the same coin for Marx. One does not exist without the other. The division of labor between the city and the countryside, for example, can rest only on private property.

> [T]he contradiction between town and country can only exist within the framework of private property. It is the most crass expression of the subjection of the individual under the division of labour, under a definite activity forced upon him—a subjugation which makes one man into a restricted town-animal, another into a restricted country-animal, and daily creates anew the conflict between their interests. Labour is here again the chief thing, power *over* individuals, and as long as this power exists, private property must exist (CW, 5, p. 64; MEW, 3, p. 50).[3]

Clearly, private property is accompanied by an involuntary division of labor which, along with private property, is to be abolished. Marx maintains that the involuntary division of labor created the possibility of contradictions within a society

> because the *division of labour* implies the possibility, nay the fact, that intellectual and material activity, that enjoyment and labour, production and consumption, devolve on different individuals, and that the only possibility of their not coming into contradiction lies in negating in its turn the division of labour (CW, 5, p. 45; MEW, 3, p. 32).

Man is subsumed not only under a division of labor which is imposed on him, but also under a class. Being subsumed predestines his life-condition. These two conditions can be eliminated only by the abolition of private property and the involuntary division of labor (MEW, 3, p. 54). Marx argues that the communist revolution will differ from previous revolutions insofar as it will not merely create a new distribution of labor leaving the kind of activity untouched. Instead, it will be directed against the hitherto existing kind of productive activity and the involuntary division of labor[4] (MEW, 3, pp. 69-70).

It would seem that individuals under capital are freer than they were earlier because their life circumstances are more subject to chance. Exactly the opposite is the case, however, since they are more subject to impersonal forces (MEW, 3, p. 76). This point of view is in agreement with the postulate that, under capital, the division of labor is based only on the authority of free competition and not, as earlier, on a formal-legal authority. Accordingly, labor, too, competes under capital and is considered to be free. The individual is nevertheless subsumed under the division of labor and is coerced by the authority of free competition which also determines the division of labor. For the individual this division is involuntary.

> [T]he *a priori* system on which the division of labour, within the workshop, is regularly carried out, becomes in the division of labour within the society, an *a posteriori*, nature-imposed necessity, controlling the lawless caprice of the producers, and perceptible in the barometrical fluctuations of the market-prices. Division of labour within the workshop implies the undisputed authority of the capitalist over men, that are but parts of a mechanism that belongs to him. The division of labour within the society brings into contact independent commodity-producers, who acknowledge no other authority but that of competition, of the coercion exerted by the pressure of their mutual interests (C1, p. 336; MEW, 23, p. 377; see also MEW, G, p. 484).

A logical consequence of this is that "Labour *is* free in all civilised countries; it is not a matter of freeing labour but of abolishing it" (CW, 5, p. 205; MEW, 3, p. 186).

In the origin of private property and commodity exchange, Marx also saw the origin of an involuntary division of labor. The involuntary division of labor spans all human history past the point at which the division of labor was based merely on sex, age, and physical strength. His writings in the *Grundrisse* (MEW, G, pp. 369-374, 484), as elsewhere (for example, MEW, 23, pp. 93-94), illustrate this with regard to precapitalist societies.

This emphasis on the involuntary nature of the division of labor is directly juxtaposed to the need to have a voluntary division of labor.

And finally, the division of labour offers us the first example of the fact that, as long as man remains in naturally evolved society, that is, as long as a cleavage exists between the particular and the common interest, as long, therefore as activity is not voluntarily, but naturally, divided, man's own deed becomes an alien power opposed to him, which enslaves him instead of being controlled by him. For as soon as the division of labour comes into being, each man has a particular, exclusive sphere of activity, which is forced upon him and from which he cannot escape (CW, 5, p. 47; MEW, 3, p. 33).[5]

This emphasis on the involuntary nature of the division of labor is one of our main criteria for interpreting Marx's theory of estrangement. The next section shows the absolute centrality of Marx's emphasis on the involuntary nature of the division of labor in his theory of estrangement.

INVOLUNTARY DIVISION OF LABOR AND
ITS CENTRALITY TO THE THEORY OF ESTRANGEMENT

As discussed in Chapter 2, Marx has two conceptions of human nature. First, those characteristics that distinguish man from animals biologically can be said to constitute the unchanging aspects of human nature. Man is a conscious being and can relate to others in ways that animals cannot. Second, there is for Marx that type of human nature that is historically conditioned. Although man has always been distinct from the animals on immutable biological grounds, his specific human nature, as contrasted with his general human nature, has undergone changes in history. Marx's theory of estrangement derives only from his biological definition of human nature, however. Man, according to Marx, is estranged because he is prevented from living according to his nature. Specifically, the worker is estranged from the product of his labor and the act of production because he is prevented from subjecting either of the two to his will; nonetheless, he does have a natural ability to do so; this ability distinguishes him biologically from animals and makes him specifically human. Being prevented from subjecting both the product of one's labor and the act of production to one's own will results directly in man's estrangement from himself, from nature, from his species-being, and from other men.

The worker's inability to subject both the act of production and the product of his labor to his own will indicates the presence of a coercive condition. Indeed, capital controls labor, and the worker is forced to sell his labor power if he wants to maintain his physical existence. Under capital, "labour is therefore not voluntary, but coerced; it is *forced labour*" (CW, 3, p. 274). The coercion is not simply a matter of one individual coercing another. The capitalist is only the personal agent of capital and is himself constrained by factors that lie outside his influence. Competition is one case in point. That work is coerced and not voluntary depends on factors that are beyond the control of any particular individual; these factors have become independent, alien forces. Work is coerced because the societal division of labor as such is involuntary.

In the previous sections, we have shown that Marx believes that the division of labor in society has been involuntary ever since the destruction of primitive communism. Under capital, competition became the regulator, but the involuntary nature of the division of labor was not abolished. Competition in the marketplace determines the nature of the division of labor in a society or among nations as well as in a particular industry. Although the capitalist determines what to produce and subjects the labor power and the product of labor to his will, he does so for reasons outside his control. Nevertheless, it is an alien will to which the worker is subjected and to which he must, contrary to his natural ability, subject his labor power. As a result, he, in agreement with others, cannot determine what is to be produced, how products are to be produced, and for what purposes. Man, unlike the animals, is by nature capable of doing so. Therefore, production under capital can exist only at the expense of the workers' estrangement.[6]

The involuntary nature of the division of labor is central to Marx's theory of estrangement. The common denominator of all forms of estrangement can be found in the involuntary nature of the division of labor. Because of it the worker is coerced into subjecting his labor power to an alien will. The capitalist himself must be viewed as merely an agent of capital, an actor who, although enjoying his social position, is himself constrained by the laws of the market. The division of labor, however, although the result of the actions of individuals (exchange) is generated involuntarily, thus leading to the subjection of man to an alien will.

NOTES

1. *Kennt* is translated here as "knows" rather than as "has." (See CW, 6, p. 184.)
2. For the translation given in the *Collected Works*, see CW, 6, p. 185.

3. See also MEW, 3, p. 32 for a similar statement, namely, that the division of labor is involuntary. In addition, see MEW, 3, p. 66.

4. Here Marx, as in MEW, 3, pp. 54, 77, mentions that *Arbeit* (labor) must be abolished. This does not mean that Marx envisions a leisure society without labor. On close inspection, it becomes evident that the word *Arbeit* can be substituted by "involuntary division of labor" or "involuntary labor." If man is subsumed under a division of labor, it cannot be said that his productive activity is voluntary, that is, that his labor is voluntary.

5. In the *Manuscripts,* Marx says that if man relates to his "own activity as an unfree activity, then he relates to it as an activity performed in the service, under the dominion, the coercion, and the yoke of another man" (CW, 3, pp. 278-279; MEW, EB 1.T., p. 519; translation mine; [the German *verhalten* is not optimally translated by "to treat," since "to treat" refers to the subject's perception, while "to relate" does not exclusively so.]

6. The question as to whether Marx's theory of estrangement is also applicable to precapitalist societies, in which the division of labor was also involuntary, is discussed in Chapter 8.

7

True Communism and Its Basis on a Voluntary Division of Labor

Thus far, it has been argued that Marx's theory of estrangement rests on his observation that productive activity is based on an involuntary division of labor. This emphasis is examined further on the basis of Marx's views on communism, since he suggested that communism was a desirable goal, through which man would be free from estrangement (MEW, E. 1.T., pp. 536-537). However, if communism is the desired form of social organization in which man is not estranged, we would expect—if our emphasis on the centrality of the involuntary division of labor to Marx's theory of estrangement is correct—that Marx views communism as a form of social organization based on a voluntary division of labor. When discussing the ways in which Marx envisioned communism, we will consider only those writings that deal directly with the division of labor under communism, and that might imply a form of social organization based on an involuntary division of labor. If Marx's writings reveal substantial evidence that he envisioned communism as a form of social organization based on a voluntary division of labor, our emphasis on the centrality of the involuntary division of labor to Marx's theory of estrangement will be considerably strengthened.

Whenever we refer to communism here, we do not mean that transitional form of society which Marx in his *Manuscripts* called "crude communism." Rather, we mean "true communism," or that form of social organization which Marx perceived to be the most ideal. At this point, it is immaterial whether Marx's communism is realizable or whether it remains a utopia. This is a totally different question. Marx's vision of communism is of importance here because it helps isolate the basis and properties of his theory of estrangement. The reader is therefore advised to suspend his questions concerning the realizability of Marx's vision of communism and to take what Marx has to say on the subject of communism as an aid in deciphering Marx's thought in general and his theory of estrangement in particular.

TRUE COMMUNISM

In the *German Ideology,* Marx proclaims that the communist revolution "removes the division of labor" (CW, 5, p. 380; MEW, 3, p. 364). What he means, of course, is that the involuntary division of labor, and not the division of labor as such, will be abolished. Neither does Marx envision communism as a society of isolated individual producers who are not subject to the coercion of the division of labor. Rather, his vision is of man cooperating freely, and voluntarily.

Let us now picture to ourselves, by way of change, a community of free individuals, carrying on their work with the means of production in common, in which the labour-power of all the different individuals is consciously applied as the combined labour-power of the community. All the characteristics of Robinson's labour are here repeated, but with this difference, that they are social, instead of individual (C1, pp. 82-83; MEW, 23, p. 92).

This theme is reiterated in the *Critique of the Gotha Programme* in which Marx again focuses not on the division of labor as such, but on that division of labor which subjugates man.

[I]n a higher phase of communist society, after the enslaving subordination of individuals under the division of labour, and therewith also the antithesis between mental and physical labour, has vanished; after labour, from a mere means of life, has itself become the prime necessity of life; after the productive forces have also increased with

the all-round development of the individual, and all the springs of co-
operative wealth flow more abundantly—only then can the narrow
horizon of bourgeois right be fully left behind and society inscribe
on its banners: from each according to his ability, to each according
to his needs! (CGP, p. 10; MEW, 19, p. 21).

Marx does not always make an explicit connection to communism when
mentioning the voluntary division of labor and juxtaposing, as well as
preferring, it to the involuntary one. Nevertheless, the message seems to
be the same, namely, that the ideal condition is one in which the division
of labor is based on voluntary cooperation rather than a forced one (see
also MEW, 3, p. 72). For example, in the *German Ideology* (MEW, 3, p. 74)
Marx mentions that the alien forces under which the individual is subsumed can be abolished only if individuals directly subsume the division
of labor. He adds that this can be done only through the collectivity, which
will in turn allow the development of one's talents. Only through the collectivity or community of individuals can personal liberty be gained.

   In the *German Ideology,* we encounter the famous passage on the society
with an involuntary division of labor in which man is

a hunter, a fisherman, a shepherd, or a critical critic, and must remain
so if he does not want to lose his means of livelihood; whereas in communist society, where nobody has one exclusive sphere of activity but
each can become accomplished in any branch he wishes, society regulates
the general production and thus makes it possible for me to do one
thing today and another tomorrow, to hunt in the morning, fish in
the afternoon, rear cattle in the evening, criticise after dinner, just as
I have in mind, without ever becoming hunter, fisherman, shepherd
or critic (MEW, 3, p. 33; translation mine.)[1]

Marx's point of view is even carried over and applied to the arts. Here, too,
Marx criticizes the coercive nature of the involuntary division of labor and
its undesirable consequences, consequences that do not arise if the division
of labor is voluntary.

[T]he exclusive concentration of artistic talent in particular individuals,
and its suppression in the broad mass which is bound up with this, is
a consequence of division of labour. . . . In any case, with a communist

organisation of society, there disappears the subordination of the artist
to local and national narrowness, which arises entirely from the division
of labour, and also the subordination of the individual to some definite
art, making him exclusively a painter, sculptor, etc.; the very name amply
expresses the narrowness of his professional development and his dependence on division of labour. In a communist society there are no painters
but only people who engage in painting among other activities" (CW, 5,
p. 394; MEW, 3, pp. 378-379).

It can be said, then, that Marx does not only believe that under communism
the division of labor will be a voluntary one and that there will be a full and
free development of each individual (MEW, 23, p. 618). In a logically consistent manner, he concludes that "[c]ommunism deprives no man of the
power to appropriate the products of society; all that it does is to deprive
him of the power to subjugate the labour of others by means of such appropriation" (CW, 6, p. 500; MEW, 4, p. 477). Hence, what distinguishes
communism is "not the abolition of property generally, but the abolition
of bourgeois property" (CW, 6, p. 498; MEW, 4, p. 475). Again, Marx
objects not to the private appropriation of products but to that kind of
private appropriation of products which leads to the creation of an involuntary division of labor, that is, to the subjugation of the labor of others.
Later in his life, he took the same theoretical position when analyzing the
reasons why the communism of early primitive societies broke down.

When the labor of others is no longer subjugated, the exploitation of
man will also be terminated. The question that arises then is how production will occur. In *The Poverty of Philosophy,* Marx suggests that
production will be organized on the basis of consensus, thus making
coercion superfluous.

What is today the result of capital and the competition of workers
among themselves will be tomorrow, if you sever the relation between
labour and capital, an actual agreement based upon the relation between the sum of productive forces and the sum of existing needs"
(CW, 6, p. 143; MEW, 4, p. 104).

Not only is such free cooperation based on consensus devoid of coercion,
"the social relations of the individual producers, with regard both to their
labour and to its products, are in this case perfectly simple and intelligible,

and that with regard not only to production but also to distribution" (C1, p. 83; MEW, 23, p. 93). This could not be said for the bourgeois form of social organization which is based on an involuntary division of labor. In bourgeois society, as in earlier epochs, the division of labor developed behind the back, as it were, of individuals, thus preventing the social relations of the individual producers from becoming "perfectly simple and intelligible."

The exchange of products as it occurred under capitalist and precapitalist social formations will also cease to exist under communism:

> Within the co-operative society based on common ownership of the means of production, the producers do not exchange their products; just as little does the labour employed on the products appear here *as the value* of these products, as a material quality possessed by them, since now, in contrast to capitalist society, individual labour no longer exists in an indirect fashion but directly as a component part of the total labour" (CGP, p. 8; MEW, 19, p. 19).

Earlier, in *The Poverty of Philosophy,* Marx made the same point when referring to communism: "[I]n principle, there is no exchange of products—but there is the exchange of the labour which co-operates in production" (CW, 6, p. 143; MEW, 4, p. 104). The emphasis is on cooperation, and the fact that individuals are freely engaged in cooperation. In contrast, under production based on an involuntary division of labor, they are brought together by force. Again with communism as a point of reference, Marx states:

> [I]f it is assumed that all members of society are immediate workers, the exchange of equal quantities of hours of labour is possible only on conclusion that the number of hours to be spent on material production is agreed on beforehand. But such an agreement negates individual exchange (MEW, 4, p. 104).[2]

Under communism, then, individuals distribute their products but do not exchange them. Distribution occurs on the basis of need, however. According to Marx, under communism products do not become commodities through the act of exchange, nor is there any commodity production in the sense that products are specifically produced for exchange.

Without commodity production, the separation of a product's use value from its exchange value will also cease. And since exchange value—which is determined by the relative amount of labor time embodied in a given product—will be nonexistent as a category, production decisions will no longer be made on the basis of whether the relative amount of embodied labor is low enough as to realize a surplus value upon being exchanged. The production of use values will no longer depend on a product's exchange value since products will not be produced for exchange, but will be produced directly for use instead. Marx makes this point in *The Poverty of Philosophy*:

> "[I]n a future society, in which class antagonism will have ceased, in which there will no longer be any classes, use will no longer be determined by the *minimum* time of production; but the time of production devoted to an article will be determined by the degree of its social utility" (CW, 6, p. 134; MEW, 4, p. 93).

And in the *Grundrisse* he writes that

> as soon as labour in the direct form has ceased to be the great well-spring of wealth, labour time ceases and must cease to be its measure, and hence exchange value [must cease to be the measure] of use value . . . . With that, production based on exchange value breaks down (G, p. 705; MEW, G, p. 593).

Thus far, it has been shown that, for Marx, communism is a society based on a voluntary division of labor. This voluntary division of labor can be guaranteed only if property that could be used to subjugate others is held in common. In addition, the division of labor under communism can be voluntary only if products are not exchanged, although distributed differentially on the basis of need, and production is regulated on the basis of consensus with everyone freely cooperating. Since Marx's theory of estrangement comes directly from his observation that man under capital is coerced into a life-situation in which he is prevented from living according to his nature, it can be concluded that communism eliminates estrangement. Communism is the solution to estrangement because it is based on a voluntary division of labor and thus lacks the coercion responsible for man's estrangement.

There is yet another way in which Marx considers the voluntary division of labor to be crucial. If throughout the history of social life under an involuntary division of labor, man has been coerced in various ways, history, too, has not been made consciously. The conscious making of history is for Marx a logical outcome of a society based on a voluntary division of labor.

[I]n history up to the present, it is certainly likewise an empirical fact that separate individuals have, with the broadening of their activity into world-historical activity, become more and more enslaved under a power alien to them (a pressure which they have conceived of as a dirty trick on the part of the so-called world spirit, etc.), a power which has become more and more enormous and, in the last instance, turns out to be the *world market* . . . . *All-round* dependence, this primary natural form of the *world-historical* co-operation of individuals, will be transformed by this communist revolution into the control and conscious mastery of these powers, which, born of the action of men on one another, have till now over-awed and ruled men as powers completely alien to them (CW, 5, pp. 51-52; MEW, 3, p. 37).

Similarly, Marx mentions that the communistic social organization will end the subjection of production to the forces of supply and demand, since man will directly control exchange and production (MEW, 3, p. 35). "The reality which communism creates is precisely the true basis for rendering it impossible that anything should exist independently of individuals, insofar as reality is nevertheless only a product of the preceding intercourse of individuals" (CW, 5, p. 81; MEW, 3, p. 70). Thus, for Marx,

communism differs from all previous movements in that it overturns the basis of all earlier relations of production and intercourse, and for the first time consciously treats all naturally evolved premises as the creations of hitherto existing men, strips them of their natural character and subjugates them to the power of the united individuals (CW, 5, p. 81; MEW, 3, p. 70).

And in the *German Ideology* he writes that

with the community of revolutionary proletarians . . . who take their conditions of existence and those of all members of society under their control . . . it is as individuals that the individuals participate in it. For it is the association of individuals (assuming the advanced stage of modern productive forces, of course) which puts the conditions of the free development and movement of individuals under their control—conditions which were previously left to chance and had acquired an independent existence over against the separate individuals precisely because of their separation as individuals and because their inevitable association, which determined the division of labour, had, as a result of their separation, become for them an alien bond (CW, 5, p. 80; MEW, 3, pp. 74-75).

We have been investigating the various ways in which Marx views social organization under communism. Not only has it become apparent that Marx directly views communism to be founded on a voluntary division of labor, it is also the case that Marx's overall vision of life under communism does not contradict the thesis that, for Marx, the voluntary division of labor is central when it comes to communism. Thus, Marx's views of the distribution and ownership of products under communism, as well as his theory of history, are directly derived from the postulate that communism is based on a voluntary division of labor. What has emerged is that as the involuntary division of labor is central to Marx's theory of estrangement, the voluntary division of labor envisioned under communism is central to Marx's vision of a world without estrangement. Therefore, we find that our emphasis on the centrality of the involuntary division of labor to Marx's theory of estrangement is justified and that our argument is considerably strengthened.

COMMUNISM AS THE ELIMINATION OF THE CONFLICT BETWEEN THE INDIVIDUAL AND THE GROUP

Marx's vision of the ideal life as one in which there is a voluntary division of labor implies that individuals are coerced neither by other individuals nor groups of individuals. This is not to say that individuals will not have conflicts of interest under communism. Marx explicitly states that individuals will cooperate on the basis of consensus; production and distribution will occur upon agreement. What is particular to Marx's vision of communism is the fact that, although differences of interest may occur, they are overcome by consensus free of coercion. He argues against those who, following Max Stirner, see social life in general as a struggle between general and personal interests (CW, 5, p. 245; MEW, 3, p. 228). Marx says that "the communists by no means want, as Saint Max believes, . . . to do away with the 'private individual' for the sake of the 'general', selfless man" (CW, 5, p. 247; MEW, 3, p. 229).

> [c]ommunist theoreticians, the only communists who have time to devote to the study of history, are distinguished precisely by the fact that they alone have *discovered* that throughout history the "general interest" is created by individuals who are defined as "private persons". They know that this contradiction is only a *seeming* one because one side of it, what is called the "general interest", is constantly being produced by the other side, private interest, and in relation to the latter it is by no means an independent force with an independent history—so that this contradiction is in practice constantly destroyed and reproduced. Hence it is not a question of the Hegelian "negative unity" of two sides of a contradiction, but of the materially determined destruction of the preceding materially determined mode of life of individuals, with the disappearance of which this contradiction together with its unity also disappears (CW, 5, p. 247; MEW, 3, p. 229).[3]

Accordingly, those who view the subject of private versus general interest as not determined by history have great difficulty in understanding the communists.

> *[C]ommunism* is quite incomprehensible to our saint because the communists do not oppose egoism to selflessness or selflessness to egoism, nor do they express this contradiction theoretically either in its sentimental or in its highflown ideological form; they rather demonstrate its material source, with which it disappears of itself (CW, 5, p. 247; MEW, 3, p. 229).

This material force consists of the continuous development of the human forces of production. This development of "the capacities of the human species takes place at the cost of the majority of human individuals and even classes, in the end it breaks through this contradiction and coincides with the development of the individual" (TS 2, p. 118;

MEW, 26.2, p. 111).[4] Hence, for Marx, communism can be founded only after productivity has reached a certain level. Productivity, defined as the time needed to produce a given product, facilitates the creation of a society in which individuals freely cooperate and in which there is no longer any struggle between personal and general interests. Historically speaking, then, Marx's vision of a society based on a voluntary division of labor can be realized only if the foundations for it have been laid in man's increased alternatives through increased productivity. This increase in alternatives is for Marx a necessary condition for the existence of a society in which the development of "the capacities of the human species . . . coincides with the development of the individual."

For Marx, another condition must be present for the abolition of the conflict between personal and general interests. Marx sees communism accompanied by a change in the consciousness of individuals. In the *German Ideology,* he writes that in communism

> we are . . . concerned with individuals at a definite historical stage of development and by no means merely with individuals chosen at random, even disregarding the indispensable communist revolution, which itself is a general condition for their free development. The individuals' consciousness of their mutual relations will, of course, likewise be completely changed, and, therefore, will no more be the "principle of love" or *dévoûment* than it will be egoism (CW, 5, p. 439; MEW, 3, p. 425).[5]

Since the "principle of love" or *dévoûment* will exist as little as the notion of egoism, it must be inferred that under communism individuals will no longer perceive such dichotomies as personal versus general interest which are so characteristic of societies with private property, that is, with an involuntary division of labor. In contrast, it can now be reiterated what communism, for Marx, is not.

Although communism enables individuals to associate freely, it cannot be conceived of as providing *the* social environment conducive to the peculiarities of an individual. Thus, individuals cannot be compared with a plant which, in order to grow, must be provided by nature with water, soil, sunshine, and the like. Communism must not be envisioned as a society in which each individual has a claim to be nurtured according to the peculiarity of his person. Marx gives the following criticism of the group who called themselves the true socialist:

The demand for a true socialist society is based on the imaginary
demand of a coco-nut palm that the "totality of life" should furnish
it with "soil, warmth, sun, air and rain" at the North Pole. This claim
of the individual on society is not deduced from the real development
of society but from the alleged relationship of the metaphysical
characters—individuality and universality. You have only to interpret single individuals as representatives, embodiments of individuality,
and society as the embodiment of universality, and the whole trick
is done. And at the same time Saint-Simon's statement about the
free development of the capacities has been correctly expressed and
placed upon its true foundation. This correct expression consists in
the absurd statement that the individuals forming society want to
preserve their "peculiarity", want to remain as they are, while they
demand of society a transformation which can only proceed from a
transformation *of themselves"* (CW, 5, p. 476; MEW, 3, pp. 464-465).

THE DEVELOPMENT OF THE INDIVIDUAL

Not only an analysis of Marx's vision of communism can show that
Marx considered estrangement to be the result of an involuntary division
of labor; the postulate that the involuntary nature of the division of
labor is central to his theory of estrangement can also be shown to be
valid with regard to his views on the development of the individual. The
individual is seen to be at his highest level of development when the
dichotomy between necessary labor and disposable time, that is free
time, no longer exists.

Marx pointed out the importance of increased spare time in several
works. He agrees with Ricardo's postulate that "wealth is disposable
time, and nothing more" (MEW, 26.3, p. 252). For Marx, disposable
time is time for the free development of the individual (MEW, G, p. 527).
The individual can spend free time in such a way as to be free from any
coercion that normally accompanies necessary labor time, that is, the
time necessarily spent in the service of a capitalist in order to make a
livelihood. Under capital, however, as a result of the capitalist's appropriation of surplus value, disposable time is unequally distributed. The worker works more hours than he is compensated for, thus allowing the capitalist to lead a life of leisure. The capitalist does not need to spend necessary
time in order to have a livelihood (MEW, G, p. 527). He is, however, interested in reducing the worker's disposable time because of his need to

increase the surplus value, that is, the time for which the worker receives no compensation.

> [A] part from extremely elastic bounds, the nature of the exchange of commodities itself imposes no limit to the working-day, no limit to surplus-labour. The capitalist maintains his rights as a purchaser when he tries to make the working-day as long as possible, and to make, whenever possible, two working-days out of one. On the other hand, the peculiar nature of the commodity sold implies a limit to its consumption by the purchaser, and the labourer maintains his right as seller when he wishes to reduce the working-day to one of definite normal duration. There is here, therefore, an antinomy, right against right, both equally bearing the seal of the law of exchanges. Between equal rights force decides. Hence is it that in the history of capitalist production, the determination of what is a working-day presents itself as the result of a struggle, a struggle between collective capital, i.e., the class of capitalists, and collective labour, i.e., the working-class (C1, p. 225; MEW, 23, p. 249).

Marx considers the outcome of this struggle important:

> Time is the room of human development. A man who has no free time to dispose of, whose whole lifetime, apart from the mere physical interruptions by sleep, meals, and so forth, is absorbed by his labour for the capitalist, is less than a beast of burden (WPP, pp. 67-68; MEW, 16, p. 144).

As a consequence, Marx approves of the legally limited working-day since it "shall make clear 'when the time which the worker sells is ended, and when his own begins'." He exclaims "Quantum mutatus ab illo!" (C1, p. 286; MEW, 23, p. 320). For Marx the working-day should be clearly limited because it increases, or at least makes possible, the planned use of one's disposable time for one's own purposes. In this regard Marx cites Engels who writes that the Ten Hours Act the worker "is enabled to prearrange his own minutes for his own purposes." He shares Engels' hope that since the factory acts have made the workers masters of their own time, they have been given "a moral energy which is directing them to the eventual possession of political power" (C1, p. 286; MEW, 23, p. 320).

The importance of the struggle for disposable time can be summed up by a passage from *Capital*:

> The intensity and productiveness of labour being given, the time which society is bound to devote to material production is shorter, and as a consequence, the time at its disposal for the free development, intellectual and social, of the individual is greater, in proportion as the work is more and more evenly divided among all the able-bodied members of society, and as a particular class is more and more deprived of the power to shift the natural burden of labour from its own shoulders to those of another layer of society. In this direction, the shortening of the working-day finds at last a limit in the generalisation of labour. In capitalist society spare time is acquired for one class by converting the whole life-time of the masses into labour-time (C1, p. 496; MEW, 23, p. 552).[6]

The increase of spare time is important because, for at least a part of the day, the worker is not subject to direct domination. Marx, therefore, sees the struggle for disposable time as one that enhances the condition in which man will be free from domination by other men, including by social forces alien to him. It is a struggle in which Marx sees an attempt to escape the involuntary division of labor. In its place should come a society based on a voluntary division of labor and devoid of the dichotomy between free time and necessary labor time. For this to occur, Marx postulates the necessity of historical development. It will be recalled that Marx considered the individual in primitive communistic societies to be still "tied" to the community as an unborn infant is tied to the mother through the umbilical cord. Of the Asian social formations, based on property held in common he says that they remained stable because, among other things, "the individual does not become independent vis-à-vis the commune." For this reason, even though individuals may have spare time at their disposal, the availability of free time to individuals is merely a necessary but not sufficient condition.

> Suppose now such an eastern bread-cutter requires 12 working-hours a week for the satisfaction of all his wants. Nature's direct gift to him is plenty of leisure time. Before he can apply this leisure time productively for himself, a whole series of historical events is required (C1, p. 482; MEW, 23, p. 538).[7]

The historical events of which Marx speaks are those events that will increase man's productive powers, although they may occur at the expense of his spare time. Marx makes the assumption that as long as man does not adequately control nature, the options for his individual development, as well as that of society, are limited, although spare time may be relatively abundant. While the productive powers are being developed, the foundations are laid not only to bring nature increasingly under man's control, but also to enable the individual to cooperate freely. The goal is both to sever the umbilical cord by which primitive man is tied to society and to shake loose all forms of social domination that have accompanied man as the development of the productive powers has proceeded throughout history. Again, as with communism, the true development of the individual is possible only if the productive powers of man are developed sufficiently and the involuntary division of labor is abolished; if man is less subject to the blind forces of nature; and if he can live free from the coercion of other men. For example:

> In fact, the realm of freedom actually begins only where labour which is determined by necessity (Not) and by external expediency (äussere Zweckmässigkeit) ceases; thus in the very nature of things it lies beyond the sphere of actual material production. Just as the savage must wrestle with nature to satisfy his wants, to maintain and reproduce life, so must civilised man, and he must do so in all social formations and under all possible modes of production. With his development this realm of physical necessity expands as a result of his wants; but, at the same time, the forces of production which satisfy these wants also increase. Freedom in this field can only consist in socialised man, the associated producers, rationally regulating their interchange with nature, bringing it under their common control, instead of being ruled by it as by a blind force (als von einer blinden Macht); and achieving this with the least expenditure of energy and under conditions most favorable to, and worthy of, their human nature. But it nonetheless still remains a realm of necessity. Beyond it begins that development of human energy which is an end in itself, the true realm of freedom, which, however, can blossom forth only with this realm of necessity as its basis. The shortening of the working-day is its basic prerequisite (MEW, 25, p. 828; translation mine).[8]

Clearly, as is pointed out above, Marx sees the shortened working-day as an important step in the struggle for a society devoid of an involuntary division of labor. The struggle is aided[9] by the tendency in the capitalist mode of production to reduce the labor time needed to produce commodities and thus increase the productivity. Under capital, this tendency is desirable because it results in a greater surplus which the capitalist can appropriate. With the abolition of the capitalist mode of production, production is no longer based on "the reduction of necessary labour time so as to posit surplus labour" (G, p. 706). Rather, there will be a "general reduction of the necessary labour of society to a minimum, which then corresponds to the artistic, scientific etc. development of the individuals in the time set free, and with the means created, for all of them" (G, p. 706; MEW, G, p. 593).

It must not therefore be concluded that a dichotomy between necessary labor and disposable time will persist in a society based on a voluntary division of labour, a society in which labor time ceases to be the measure of wealth and hence, in which "exchange value [must cease to be the measure] of use value" (G, p. 705). Neither must it be assumed that, if capitalism is no longer a reality, productivity gains could no longer be realized. The facts are quite the contrary. For Marx, the reduction in necessary labor time to a minimum will in itself lead to an increased level of productivity.

[T]he saving of labour time [is] equal to an increase of free time, i.e., time for the full development of the individual, which in turn reacts back upon the productive power of labour as itself the greatest productive power. From the standpoint of the direct production process it can be regarded as the production of *fixed capital*, this fixed capital being man himself (G, pp. 711-712; MEW, G, p. 599).

Similarly, a maximum of disposable time feeds back upon the individuals insofar as they become transformed: "Free-time—which is both idle time and time for higher activity—has naturally transformed its possessor into a different subject, and he then enters into the direct production process as this different subject" (G, p. 712; MEW, G, p. 599). Marx suggests that "it goes without saying . . . that direct labour time itself cannot remain in the abstract antithesis to free time in which it appears from the perspective of bourgeois economy" (G, p. 712).

This theme is reiterated in *Theories of Surplus-Value*.

[I]t is self-evident that if labour-time is reduced to a normal length and, furthermore, labour is no longer performed for someone else, but for myself . . . it acquires a quite different, a free character, it becomes real social labor. . . —the labour of a man who has also disposable time must be of a much higher quality than that of the beast of burden (TS3, p. 257; MEW, 26.3, p. 253).

Marx cautions, however, that "labour cannot become play, as Fourier would like, although it remains his great contribution to have expressed the suspension not of distribution, but of the mode of production itself" (G, p. 712). Instead, Marx describes the production process under communism as a process that is

both discipline, as regards the human being in the process of becoming and, at the same time, practice [Ausübung], experimental science, materially creative and objectifying science, as regards the human being who has become, in whose head exists the accumulated knowledge of society" (G, p. 712; MEW, G, pp. 599-600).

In this discussion of Marx's vision of communism, it became evident that, for Marx, communism is a society based on a voluntary division of labor. This confirmed our postulate that the involuntary division of labor Marx observed in capitalist and many precapitalist societies is central to his theory of estrangement, since communism, for Marx, is above all a society devoid of estrangement. The centrality of the involuntary division of labor in Marx's theory of estrangement is also clear with regard to Marx's views of the development of the individual. For Marx, the true development of the individual cannot come about until the whole society is freed from the involuntary division of labor and the forces of production have been developed sufficiently. This is so even for the class which in a given society may not be forced to work for a living. Thus, just as much as the capitalist is estranged, he and society are also prevented from full and free development as long as the involuntary division of labor prevails. Marx's views on the development of the individual are, therefore, intricately related to his assessment of the consequences of the involuntary division of labor. Insofar as these views call for a voluntary division of labor such that the individual may fully and freely develop, the full development of the individual coincides with and depends on the establishment of communism. And insofar as this development can occur only in a society devoid of estrangement, it can be concluded that the centrality of the involuntary division of labor to Marx's theory of estrangement indirectly also derives from his views on the development of the individual.

DISCUSSSION

As we have seen, Marx believes that communism will be founded on and will depend on the productivity gains realized under capital. The inherent capitalist tendency to lower the amount of labor time used in the production of commodities does in fact result in a greater level of productivity. Thus, the necessary labor time can be set to a minimum while maximizing the amount of free time. However, this very maximization of free time will lead to further productivity increases.[10] An increase in productivity therefore represents a step in the direction of eliminating scarcity, particularly in Marx's vision of a communist society in which exploitation ceases to exist. The question that arises is whether communist society will be free from scarcity. There is no evidence showing that Marx believed communist society will be, or even could be, devoid of any scarcity. Even under communism, man will have to work for his maintenance as well as for that of his offspring.

Scarcity is a major point of discussion in Knecht's work. In his comparison of Sartre's and Marx's theory of estrangement, Knecht (1975) points out that Sartre's theory of estrangement is more broadly conceived than Marx's.[11] Sartre deliberately set out to establish a theory of estrangement that would not be bound to and derived from specific historical conditions. His theory rests on the assumption that scarcity does exist and that it exists independent of any socioeconomic organization. Because of this scarcity, with which individuals must cope, individuals become estranged in the process. As a consequence, Sartre also tends to view social organization as a means of coping with scarcity which results in the estrangement of the individual. Thus, because of scarcity one man appears to the other as a coercive "anti-man," in any historical period and in all human relationships, including the family and the community of friends (Knecht, 1975: 87). According to Sartre, estrangement can be eliminated only if scarcity is overcome. However, while Sartre does not state that scarcity will never be overcome, he does maintain that estrangement can slowly be reduced even under scarcity (Knecht, 1975: 98).

Although Marx does not assume the end of scarcity under communism, he is not as concerned about it as Sartre and does not cite it as the basic cause of past or future estrangement. Sartre incessantly pursues the problem of estrangement from the point of view of how the individual will directly or indirectly experience interference from other individuals, because of the underlying phenomenon of scarcity. Marx, however, assumes that communism will be accompanied by a change in consciousness. "We are . . . concerned with individuals at a definite historical stage of development and by no means merely with individuals chosen at random," he says. Thus, Marx, while not assuming the absence of scarcity, is able to say that under communism the development of the forces of production "coincides with the development of the individual." Since "the individuals' consciousness of their mutual relations will . . . be completely changed," and production and distribution will be based on agreement with everyone participating freely, Marx does not believe scarcity results in renewed estrangement. He thinks that the consciousness of individuals under communism will constantly identify the development of individuals with that of society. Sartre sees this unity as unstable, although he does envision situations in which a group of individuals cooperate freely without the coercion of anyone. Such a group, Sartre argues, can be a collectivity of individuals involved in storming the Bastille, or any other group with homogeneous goals (Knecht, 1975: 210). However, as a result of the persisting scarcity, such groups are unstable and tend to become coercive. Thus, Knecht (1975: 274) writes that scarcity is the direct cause of the failure of associations previously free from estrangement.

Sartre can visualize situations in which the consciousness of individuals would be so changed that a group could achieve homogeneity with respect to its members' goal-directedness. All the same, he is certain that this change is not likely to persist in the long run. It may therefore be concluded that Sartre, although admitting some historical influences on individuals, excludes others. For example, the associated individuals involved in the storming of the Bastille were subject to definite historical influences bringing about that change in consciousness leading to the uncoerced cooperation in storming the Bastille. Unlike Marx, Sartre would not postulate that the establishment of communist society would bring about a change in consciousness so persistent that, despite the continuous presence of scarcity, estrangement would never reappear. Sartre may there-fore be accused of basing his theory of estrangement on a concept of the individual that is not sufficiently historic. Such a claim could be substantiated by the fact that his theory of estrangement is derived not from historical categories but from the principle of scarcity, which in itself is assumed to be independent of historical conditions. For Sartre, scarcity is a reality of life transcending historical periods (Knecht, 1975). Accordingly, contrary to Marx, estrangement is not seen as a phenomenon associated with dis-tinct historical phases. Although estrangement may be overcome, once overcome it is not assumed that this overcoming, while in itself an event of history, will receive history's "seal of guarantee" as Marx tended to postulate. As one example of the way in which Marx links the abolition of estrangement to a definite historical period, the following pronounce-ment from the *Manifesto* may be cited: "In place of the old bourgeois society, with its classes and class antagonisms, we shall have an associa-tion, in which the free development of each is the condition for the free development of all" (CW, 6, p. 506; MEW, 4, p. 482).

For Marx, this can only be the consequence of a revolution introducing a new historical epoch. By means of a revolution, the proletariat "makes itself the ruling class, and, as such, sweeps away by force the old condi-tions of production, then it will, along with these conditions, have swept away the conditions for the existence of class antagonisms and of classes generally, and will thereby have abolished its own supremacy as a class" (CW, 6, p. 506; MEW, 4, p. 482).

Unlike Sartre, Marx envisions communist society as stable inasmuch as estrangement will not reoccur. History will have changed both the con-sciousness of individuals and the form of social organization so as to "guarantee" nonestrangement. According to this view, the relationship of the individual to society is "deduced from the real development of society," and not the alleged relationship of the metaphysical characters—individuality and universality" (CW, 5, p. 476; MEW, 3, p. 464).

Marx also refuses to neglect the historical context. Because Marx sees the relationship of the individual to society within primitive societies in historical terms, it is incorrect to assume, as Hobbes tended to do, that a strong individual will begin to dominate weaker ones. To make such an assumption, says Marx, is to start with a notion of isolated individuals, and not with the individual that is historically linked to other individuals in specific ways.

Marx admits that "there is no natural obstacle absolutely preventing one man from disburdening himself of the labour requisite for his own existence, and burdening another with it, any more, for instance, than unconquerable natural obstacles prevent one man from eating the flesh of another" (C1, p. 479). A general pattern of domination will occur only with an initial development of the productiveness of labor:

> It is only after men have raised themselves above the rank of animals, when therefore their labour has been to some extent socialised, that a state of things arises in which the surplus-labour of the one becomes a condition of existence for the other (C1, p. 479; MEW, 23, pp. 534-535).

The historical conditions are, therefore, extremely important in explaining the behavior of individuals. Just as social relations change in history, so does consciousness. According to Marx, the perception of an antimony between the private and the general interest is also historically conditioned and is directly linked to the institution of private property. Hence, it is only natural that he assumes that different historical conditions (for example, those of primitive society or communism) will produce different social relations and a different consciousness of mutual relations in the individuals. Just as the domination of some over others was unlikely in primitive society, Marx thinks it unlikely that estrangement will recur under communism and that some will again begin to dominate others. The condition of nonestrangement under communism is for Marx—and in contrast to Sartre—stable.

That Marx views communism as a society with no reemergence of estrangement can be illustrated in yet another way. As has been shown, Marx sees communism as a type of society in which products are distributed on the basis of need. The unequal accumulation of personal property and the subsequent exchange of such accumulated property brought about the downfall of primitive communism as exemplified by the Iroquois Indians. As Engels remarked, this process brought the Iroquois to the threshold of civilization. On the basis of this initial regular exchange, the division of labor and private property arose. The division of labor developed and grew

without the consent of the individuals involved. Under communism, however, there is no room for the exchange of products and commodity production. Marx believes that the "mechanisms" that transformed primitive
communist society and propelled history ever since will cease to exist
and will not reemerge since production will no longer be based on exchange
value but on agreement with products being collectively appropriated and
distributed on the basis of need. Hence, history will be consciously directed
history, and the division of labor will cease to be formed independently of
the will of individuals:

> The reality which communism creates is precisely the true basis for
> rendering it impossible that anything should exist independently of
> individuals, insofar as reality is nevertheless only a product of the pre-
> ceding intercourse of individuals (CW, 5, p. 81; MEW, 3, p. 70).

> In history up to the present it is certainly likewise an empirical fact
> that separate individuals have . . . become more and more enslaved
> under a power alien to them . . . a power which has become more and
> more enormous and, in the last instance, turns out to be the *world
> market* . . . *All-round* dependence, this primary natural form of the
> *world-historical* co-operation of individuals, will be transformed by
> this communist revolution into the control and conscious mastery
> of these powers, which, born of the action of men on one another,
> have till now overawed and ruled men as powers completely alien to
> them (CW, 5, p. 51; MEW, 3, p. 37; see also MEW, 3, p. 35).

For Marx communism is not the end of history. Rather, it is the beginning of a new type of history—consciously directed history[12]. It is made
possible by the elimination of "mecahnisms" such as exchange, commodity production, and the resulting involuntary division of labor which
hitherto propelled it. As long as these "mechanisms" are absent, Marx
sees no reason to believe that communism will be an unstable social condition despite the presence of some scarcity. In this respect, Marx differs
from Sartre.

The question may be asked now whether Marx also perceived man
under the communism of primitive societies to be free from estrangement.
It may be recalled that Marx and Engels thought these individuals were free

from coercion by others and were therefore not subject to the involuntary division of labor to be introduced only after exchange relationships have emerged. Consequently, Marx does not speak of estrangement or alien social forces dominating man in primitive communistic societies. If estrangement results from an involuntary division of labor, which in itself is a product of society, it must be concluded that, for Marx, man in primitive communistic societies is not estranged. Nonetheless, he does not consider this condition, primitive communism, to be desirable because man is still severely under the domination of nature and tied to his community as if through an umbilical cord. Only with the introduction of regular exchange does man first sever his symbiotic ties to the community and develop the forces of production that will eventually allow the realization of communism. Thus, while man cannot be said to be estranged under primitive communism, he is incapable of that type of life envisioned under communism since neither society nor the individual have yet become developed. The development of man's productive powers and the individual has resulted in estrangement. Until a certain level of development has occurred, increases in the productive powers of man are for Marx only possible through estrangement. If, therefore, the development of the forces of production helps man bring nature under greater control (although resulting in estrangement), scarcity is in part overcome at the price of estrangement, at least for certain historical periods.[13] At the price of estrangement, man increases his alternatives vis-à-vis nature and, therefore, develops himself as well as diminishes scarcity.[14]

Scarcity must not be seen primarily as an independent variable definable in ahistorical terms. For Marx, scarcity also seems to be closely linked with the level of individual development. Historically, as the individual develops, new needs are created, and what is considered to be scarce may change because of certain historical developments. This cannot be said of animals whose needs are physiologically derivable and, therefore, not subject to historical change. Needs are ahistorically determinable with animals:

> The different forms of material life are, of course, in every case dependent on the needs which are already developed, and the production, as well as the satisfaction, of these needs in an historical process, which is not found in the case of a sheep or a dog. (CW, 5, p. 82; MEW, 3, p. 71).

In *Capital* Marx points out that "at the dawn of civilization the productiveness acquired by labour is small, but so too are the wants which develop with and by the means of satisfying them" (C1, p. 479; MEW, 23, p. 535[15]; see also quote in note 9; MEW, 25, p. 828).

For Marx, then, the development of man's productive powers is initially accompanied by estrangement. This development proceeds under communism in the absence of estrangement. However, only if necessary labor time can sufficiently be reduced by the development of productive forces is communism perceived to be realizable.

> [The] development of productive forces . . . is an absolutely necessary practical premise, because without it privation, *want* is merely made general, and with *want* the struggle for necessities would begin again, and all the old filthy business would necessarily be restored (CW, 5, p. 49; MEW, 3, pp. 34-35).[16]

The reduction of necessary labor time can be equated with a reduction in scarcity or an increased satisfaction of needs. However, because new needs are created as the forces of production develop, scarcity remains a relative concept not solely definable according to physiological premises. Scarcity, along with needs, can therefore be said to be created as the productive powers of man develop. On the whole, the productive forces are thought to develop faster so that under communism man can minimize the necessary labor time and establish a society based on a voluntary division of labor. Some scarcity will still be present, even if only because nature can never be fully controlled.

"Just as the savage must wrestle with Nature to satisfy his wants, to maintain and reproduce life, so must civilized man, and he must do so in all social formations and under all possible modes of production" (C3, p. 820; MEW, 25, p. 828). Here Marx apparently contradicts a position he took earlier. In the *Manuscripts,* he says that man, in contrast to animals, "produces even when he is free from physical need and only truly produces in freedom therefrom" (CW, 3, p. 276; MEW, EB 1.T., p. 517). Considering his work as a whole, it seems that Marx did not equate "true productive activity" with that activity which occurs free from physical need. Rather, he envisioned a society in which production would occur on the basis of freely cooperating individuals regardless of the basis for this cooperation. Thus, as long as man is able to satisfy his physical needs without being dominated by an alien will, he is not estranged and the division of labor is a voluntary one.

Marx does accept the fact that man is "determined, forced," by his needs, but he is quick to add that in this case "it is only my own nature . . . which exerts force upon me; it is nothing alien." Only if production is determined on the basis of exchange do my needs become a coercive force for others as well (G, p. 245; MEW, G, p. 157). Again, it can be seen that Marx's main emphasis is on the *way* needs are satisfied, not on the idea that man must produce in order to satisfy his needs. For Marx, communism is that form of social organization in which man is capable of producing, without coercion, the products required to satisfy his needs, since neither production nor distribution rests on exchange and the division of labor is voluntary.

MARX'S DEFINITION OF HUMAN NATURE RECONSIDERED

According to Marx, communism is not a society in which the individuals forming that society "want to preserve their 'peculiarity', while they demand of society a transformation which can only proceed from a transformation of themselves." Marx does not outline what human nature will be under communism. He is not concerned with human nature as it manifests itself in the various types of behavior and characters of individuals living under communism. He often criticizes those who, by extrapolating from behavior under capital, claimed to have found the ingredients of human nature. This criticism was intended to relativize statements about human nature which others thought to be absolute, and not to explicitly outline human nature under communism.

Marx was very concerned about human nature in another way. Earlier, we stated that Marx's theory of estrangement was derived from a biological, and not an historical, conception of human nature. Thus, man, unlike the animals, was found to be a producer capable of producing according to his will, and insofar as man is forced to subject his labor power and the product of his labor to an alien will he can be said to be estranged. Marx depicts communism as society without estrangement, a society in which neither one's labor power nor the product of one's labor is subject to an alien will. Cooperation is free and the division of labor voluntary. Communism therefore permits man to live according to his nature, a nature based not on characteristics that may change in history but one that is biologically unique to man.

NOTES

1. The translation is mine insofar as *wie ich gerade Lust habe* is translated by "as I have in mind" rather than by "as I have a mind," as it appears in CW, 5, p. 47.

2. Marx uses the term *immédiat* (*travailleurs immédiats*), which can be translated by "immediate." However, *immédiat* designates the condition of someone *qui agit, qui produit sans intermédiaire*. (See Walther v. Wartburg, *Französisches Etymologisches Wörterbuch*, Basel: Helbing & Lichtenbahn, 1952, p. 571).

3. Marx criticizes not only those who see a conflict between the private and the general interest from a historical perspective, but also those who see no such divergence as long as the individuals in an exchange society are allowed to pursue their private interests.

The economists express this as follows: Each pursues his private interest and only his private interest; and thereby serves the private interests of all, the general interest, without willing or knowing it. The real point is not that each individual's pursuit of his private interests promotes the totality of private interests, the general interest. One could just as well deduce from this abstract phrase that each individual reciprocally blocks the assertion of the others' interests, so that, instead of a general affirmation, this war of all against all produces a general negation. The point is rather that private interest is itself already a socially determined interest, which can be achieved only within the conditions laid down by society and with the means provided by society; hence it is bound to the reproduction of these conditions and means. It is the interest of private persons; but its content as well as the form and means of its realization is given by social conditions independent of all (G, p. 156; MEW, G, p. 74).

4. Marx elaborates on this theme elsewhere. When discussing the nature of the capitalist, he says that

fanatically bent on making value expand itself, he ruthlessly forces the human race to produce for production's sake; he thus forces the development of the productive powers of society, and creates those material conditions, which alone can form the real basis of a higher form of society, a society in which the full and free development of every individual forms the ruling principle (C1, p. 555; MEW, 23, p. 618; see also MEW, 19, p. 17; MEW, G, p. 716, and MEW, 3, p. 424).

5. In the *Grundrisse,* Marx uses the same argument when discussing the reasons why in primitive society a strong individual did not dominate weaker ones and thus forcefully extract labor from them.

> It is of course very simple to imagine that some powerful, physically dominant individual, after first having caught the animal, then catches humans in order to have them catch animals; in a word, uses human beings as another naturally occurring condition for his reproduction (whereby his own labour reduces itself to ruling) like any other natural creature. But such a notion is stupid—correct as it may be from the standpoint of some particular given clan or commune—because it proceeds from the development of *isolated Individuals.* But human beings become individuals (vereinzelt) through the process of history (G, p. 496; MEW, G, p. 395).

Implicit in this statement is the postulate that it is inconceivable for a "primitive" individual even to consider perceiving his interest to be prior to the one of others, that is, to subordinate others to his will in such a manner that he benefits from the subordination. At this point, we should also recall that Marx did not explain the decay of primitive communism by the fact that some began to dominate others by virtue of personal physical strength. Rather, he explained it on the basis that personal property was unequally appropriated leading to social processes, as a result of which some became the subordinates of others.

6. In *Theories of Surplus-Value,* Marx maintains the same theme in a somewhat more arithmetic form:

> Assume that the productivity of industry is so advanced that whereas earlier two-thirds of the population were directly engaged in material production, now it is only one-third. Previously 2/3 produced means of subsistence for 3/3; now 1/3 produce for 3/3. Previously 1/3 was net revenue (as distinct from the revenue of the labourers), now 2/3. Leaving (class) contradictions out of account, the nation would now use 1/3 of its time for direct production, where previously it needed 2/3. Equally distributed, the whole 2/3 would have more time for unproductive labour and leisure (MEW, 26.1, p. 189; translation mine).

The Progress Publishers' translation (TS1, p. 218) translates the last sentence in the following way: "Equally distributed, all (that is, the whole population) would have 2/3 more time for unproductive labour and leisure." This translation cannot be correct because of the arithmetic. If a population previously spent one-third of its time as spare time (while two-thirds were needed to produce subsistence), it now has two-thirds in the form of spare time, while only one-third of the time is used for the direct production of subsistence. The spare time increased by 100 percent and not, as the translation implies, by 66-1/3 percent. The German "Gleichmässig verteilt, hätten alle 2/3 mehr Zeit" is therefore best translated as "Equally distributed, the whole 2/3 would have more time." Furthermore, if equally distributed, the capitalist class would have less—not more—spare time than previously, since it, too, must now spend one-third of its time producing means of subsistence.

7. Marx continues by saying that "before he spends it in surplus-labour for strangers, compulsion is necessary. If capitalist production were introduced, the honest fellow would perhaps have to work six days a week, in order to appropriate to himself the product of one working-day" (C1, p. 482; MEW, 23, p. 538).

8. *Äussere Zweckmässigkeit* is not optimally translated by "mundane considerations" (C3, p. 820). It implies that the worker who is uncoerced by necessity (*Not*) or by "external expediency" (*äussere Zweckmässigkeit*) has no mundane considerations. Marx's emphasis rather is on coercion brought about by *Not* or *äussere Zweckmässigkeit* and not on whether considerations are mundane or not.

The phrase *als von einer blinden Macht* is misleadingly translated in the Progress Publishers' edition by "as by the blind forces of Nature" (C3, p. 820).

In Roman society, which was based on slavery, the ties between the individual and the community were severed. While "the individuals may appear great," Marx maintains that "there can be no conception here of a free and full development either of the individual or of the society, since such development stands in contradiction to the original relation" (G, p. 487; MEW, G, pp. 386-387). Implicit here is the notion that the free and full development of the individual cannot come about unless the productive forces are sufficiently developed. Although slavery brought about a certain development, it was limited. The free and full development of the individual and society was impossible since the options, though increased, were still too limited. Also implicit here is the idea that, unless all men are free from coercion (involuntary division of labor), neither the individuals nor society can develop freely and fully even though some individuals have the spare time for their development through which in turn they may appear great.

9.

[Capital] diminishes labour time in the necessary form so as to increase it in the superfluous form; hence posits the superfluous in growing measure as a condition—question of life or death—for the necessary. On the one side, then, it calls to life all the powers of science and of nature, as of social combination and of social intercourse, in order to make the creation of wealth independent (relatively) of the labour time employed on it. On the other side, it wants to use labour time as the measuring rod for the giant social forces thereby created, and to confine them within the limits required to maintain the already created value as value. Forces of production and social relations—two different sides of the development of the social individual—appear to capital as mere means, and are merely means for it to produce on its limited foundation. In fact, however, they are the material conditions to blow this foundation sky-high. "Truly wealthy a nation, when the working day is 6 rather than 12 hours" (G, p. 706; MEW, G, pp. 593-594).

10. In *Anti-Dühring* (MEW, 20, pp. 274, 276), Engels also maintains that a society that is freed from the limits of capitalist production will be able to advance further because it creates new forces of production. This advance will be possible because abandonment of the previous division of labor and its replacement by a division of labor will allow for the education of many-sided individuals who will also understand the scientific basis of all industrial production. Quoting Marx, he points to the fact that under capital the factory system itself is already moving in such a direction:

> [T]he employment of machinery does away with the necessity of crystallizing this distribution after the manner of Manufacture, by the constant annexation of a particular man to a particular function. Since the motion of the whole system does not proceed from the workman, but from the machinery, a change of persons can take place at any time without an interruption of the work (C1, p. 397; MEW, 23, pp. 443-444).

Engels states that once the economy no longer suffers under recurrent crises and the means of production are no longer privately owned, a practically limitless increase in production will occur. In contrast to the development postulated above, the one postulated here is seen only as a function of a reduction of losses (MEW, 20, p. 263).

11. Schaff (1964:110) maintains that it is impossible, as Sartre did, to merge existentialism with Marxism. Schaff considers Sartre's attempt a failure because of the resulting inherent philosophical contradictions. (See also Schaff, 1964: 22, 26, 76, 78, 109.)

12. "For it is the association of individuals (assuming the advanced stage of modern productive forces, of course) which puts the conditions of the free development and movement of individuals under their control—conditions which were previously left to chance and had acquired an independent existence over against the separate individuals." (CW, 5, p. 80; MEW, 3, p. 75).

13. As pointed out earlier, Marx envisions the further development of the forces of production also under communism but not at the expense of estrangement.

14. Here "diminishing scarcity" means that, through the development of the forces of production, a society's necessary labor time is diminished. However, necessary labor time is in itself historically determined; what is necessary cannot be seen as invariable.

15. We note that *Bedürfnis* is translated by "want" rather than by "need." In light of Marx's use of the term *Bedürfnis*, it is difficult to justify one translation exclusively over another, although I prefer the translation "need." For a further treatment, see Agnes Heller, 1976.

16. Criticizing Max Stirner, Marx says in the *German Ideology:*

In reality, of course, what happened was that people won freedom for themselves each time to the extent that was dictated and permitted not by their
ideal of man, but by the existing productive forces. All emancipation carried
through hitherto has been based, however, on restricted productive forces.
The production which these productive forces could provide was insufficient
for the whole of society and made development possible only if some persons
satisfied their needs at the expense of others, and therefore some—the minority—
obtained the monopoly of development, while others—the majority—owing to
the constant struggle to satisfy their most essential needs, were for the time
being (i.e., until the creation of new revolutionary productive forces) excluded
from any development. Thus, society has hitherto always developed within
the framework of a contradiction—in antiquity the contradiction between free
men and slaves, in the Middle Ages that between nobility and serfs, in modern
times that between the bourgeoisie and the proletariat (CW, 5, p. 431-432;
MEW, 3, p. 417).

8

IS ESTRANGEMENT LIMITED
TO CAPITALIST SOCIETIES?

If the foregoing interpretation of Marx, with its emphasis on the involuntary nature of the division of labor, is correct, it would have to be concluded that man is estranged whenever an involuntary division of labor exists. Such a conclusion would be the logical consequence of a theory that postulates estrangement to result from the involuntary nature of the division of labor and that assumes the lack of any estrangement under communism because of the absence of such a division of labor. In this chapter, instead of merely drawing the logical consequences, the attempt is made to investigate Marx's views on precapitalist, noncommunistic societies in order to determine whether such a conclusion holds up and how the conclusion can be termed valid.

ESTRANGEMENT AND PRECAPITALISTIC, NONPRIMITIVE SOCIETIES

Marx thinks the division of labor became involuntary following the destruction of the communism of primitive societies. This belief is more concretely expressed in Marx's discussion of the nature of the master-servant relation (*Herrschaftsverhältnis*):

Basically the appropriation of animals, land etc. cannot take place
in a master-servant relation, although the animal provides service.
The presupposition of the master-servant relation is the appropriation of an alien *will* (G, pp. 500-501; MEW, G, p. 400).

In the master-servant relation, the same condition is given as under
capital; namely, that labor power is subject to an alien will and is no
longer directed by the will of the individual who exerts this power. The
master can appropriate an alien will because of his ownership of the
land[1] and the resulting dependency of others on him:

> [F]eudal landed property is already by its very nature huckstered
> land—the earth which is estranged from man and hence confronts
> him in the shape of a few great lords. The domination of the land
> as an alien power over men is already inherent in feudal landed
> property. The serf is the adjunct of the land (CW, 3, p. 266; MEW,
> EB 1.T., p. 505).

Under precapitalist servitude, just as under capital, the serf and his labor
power are subject to an alien will, and at least a portion of the product
of labor is appropriated by the master. This action can be seen as a violation of human nature since, for Marx, man is by nature capable of consciously directing productive activity with his will and also of subjecting
the product of his labor to his volition. Under servitude, as under capital,
this condition is not given, and man is prevented from living according to
his nature. Man must therefore emancipate himself from all servitude
(*Knechtschaftsverhältnisse*), the most recent of which is that of capital:

> From the relationship of estranged labour to private property it fol-
> lows further that the emancipation of society from private property,
> etc., from servitude, is expressed in the *political* form of the *emancipa-
> tion of the workers;* not that *their* emancipation alone is at stake, but
> because the emancipation of the workers contains universal human
> emancipation—and it contains this, because the whole of human servi-
> tude is involved in the relation of the worker to production, and all
> relations of servitude are but modifications and consequences of this
> relation (CW, 3, p. 280; MEW, EB 1.T., p. 521).

Marx's analysis of precapitalist economic formations goes beyond the narrowest definition of the master-servant relationship. Nevertheless, the individuals who are in any way dependent remain unfree for him:

> It is furthermore evident that in all forms in which the direct labourer remains the "possessor" of the means of production and labour conditions necessary for the production of his own means of subsistence, the property relationship must simultaneously appear as a direct relation of lordship and servitude, so that the direct producer is not free; a lack of freedom which may be reduced from serfdom with enforced labour to a mere tributary relationship. The direct producer, according to our assumption, is to be found here in possession of his own means of production, the necessary material labour conditions required for the realisation of his labour and the production of his means of subsistence . . . . Under such conditions the surplus-labour for the nominal owner of the land can only be extorted from them by other than economic pressure, whatever the form may be. This differs from slave or plantation economy in that the slave works under alien conditions of production and not independently. Thus, conditions of personal dependence are requisite, a lack of personal freedom, no matter to what extent, and being tied to the soil as its accessory, bondage in the true sense of the word (C3, pp. 790-791; MEW, 25, pp. 798-799).

Even though the tributary relationship implies freedom from enforced labor in which labor power is directly subsumed under an alien will, our thesis still holds. Because of an alien will, the individual is forced to expend labor power, in the form of surplus labor, for the nominal owner of the land. Against his will, he is compelled to produce a surplus he cannot appropriate. In addition, although his labor power is not directly subjected to an alien will, he is not free to produce any type of surplus. Thus, as under capital, he is free neither in deciding what total surplus is to be produced nor in appropriating all of the surplus and disposing over it. Marx describes the nature of coercion existing in this case:

> Rent in kind presupposes a higher stage of civilization for the direct producer, i.e., a higher level of development of his labour and of society in general. And it is distinct from the preceding form in that

surplus-labour needs no longer be performed in its natural form, thus no longer under the direct supervision and compulsion of the landlord or his representatives; the direct producer is driven rather by force of circumstances than by direct coercion, through legal enactment rather than the whip, to perform it on his own responsibility. Surplus-production, in the sense of production beyond the indispensable needs of the direct producer, and within the field of production actually belonging to him, upon the land exploited by himself instead of, as earlier, upon the nearby lord's estate beyond his own land, has already become a self-understood rule here. In this relation the direct producer more or less disposes of his entire labour-time, although, as previously, a part of this labour-time, at first practically the entire surplus portion of it, belongs to the landlord without compensation; except that the landlord no longer directly receives this surplus-labour in its natural form, but rather in the products' natural form in which it is realised (C3, pp. 794-795; MEW, 25, p. 803).

Speaking of the source of value and the appropriation of surplus value, Marx compares the coercion under precapitalist social formations to wage labor:

The substance of value is and remains nothing but expended labour-power. . . . A serf for instance expends his labour-power for six days, and the fact of this expenditure as such is not altered by the circumstance that he may be working three days for himself, on his own field, and three days for his lord, on the field of the latter. Both his voluntary labour for himself and his forced labour for his lord are equally labour; so far as this labour is considered with reference to the values, or to the useful articles created by it, there is no difference in his six days of labour. The difference refers merely to the different conditions by which the expenditure of his labour-power during both halves of his labour-time of six days is called forth. The same applies to the necessary and surplus-labour of the wage-labourer (C2, p. 390; MEW, 24, p. 385).

In *Theories of Surplus-Value*, he states: "Serf-labour (just as slave-labour) has this in common with wage-labour, in respect to rent, that the latter is paid in *labour* not in *products*, still less in *money*" (TS3, p. 401; MEW, 26.3, p. 392).

In general, other comments of Marx on precapitalist economic formations may be noted, particularly as they address the nature of coercion:

> Hence, the historical movement which changes the producers into wage-workers, appears, on the one hand, as their emancipations from serfdom and from the fetters of the guilds, ... But, on the other hand, these new freedmen became sellers of themselves only after they had been robbed of all their own means of production, and of all the guarantees of existence afforded by the old feudal arrangements. . . . The starting-point of the development that gave rise to the wage labourer as well as to the capitalist, was the servitude of the labourer. The advance consisted in a change of form of this servitude, in the transformation of feudal exploitation into capitalist exploitation (C1, p. 669; MEW, 23, p. 743).

And although Marx often points to the Asiatic precapitalist social formation as an example of a stable, persisting organization, resistant to the undermining forces of exchange, he is very critical of the way some surplus is appropriated through coercion:

> Rent (as the Physiocrats conceive it by *reminiscence* of feudal conditions) appears historically (and still on the largest scale among the Asiatic peoples) as the general form of *surplus labour,* of labour performed without payment in return. The appropriation of this surplus labour is here not mediated by exchange, as is the case in capitalist society, but its basis is the forcible domination of one section of society over the other. (There is, accordingly, direct slavery, serfdom or political dependence) (TS3, p. 400; MEW, 26.3, p. 391).

Although man is subject to an alien will under precapitalist economic formations, the manner in which this subjection occurs differs from capital, the main distinction being the absence of exchange as the basis of all production. In precapitalist social formations, the estranged elements of life are still bound by man and are not subject to exchange relations and the resulting competition:

> Precisely the *slavery of civil society* is in *appearance* the greatest *freedom* because it is in appearance the fully developed *independence* of the individual, who considers as his *own* freedom the uncurbed movement, no longer bound by a common bond or by man, of the estranged elements of his life, such as property, industry, religion, etc., whereas actually this is his fully developed slavery and inhumanity. *Law* has here taken the place of *privilege* (CW, 4, p. 116; MEW, 2, p. 123).

Similarly, in the *German Ideology,* Marx writes that

> in imagination, individuals seem freer under the dominance of the bourgeoisie than before, because their conditions of life seem accidental; in reality, of course, they are less free, because they are to a greater extent governed by material forces" (CW, 5, pp. 78-79; MEW, 3, p. 76).[2]

Clearly, although coercion is a fact in precapitalist societies, it increases with increased exchange relationships. It would be a mistake, however, to think that coercion was based only on personal dominance, that the estranged elements of life were bound only by man. Marx's emphasis rather is on the degree to which either personal or impersonal forces were the source of coercion which resulted in the subjection of man to an alien will:

> When we look at social relations which create an undeveloped system of exchange, of exchange values and of money, or which correspond to an undeveloped degree of these, then it is clear from the outset that the individuals in such a society, although their relations appear to be more personal, enter into connection with one another only as individuals imprisoned within a certain definition, as feudal lord and vassal, landlord and serf, etc., or as members of a caste etc. or as members of an estate etc. . . . (As regards the illusion of the "purely personal relations" in feudal times, etc., it is of course not to be forgotten for a moment (1) that these relations, in a certain phase, also took on an objective character within their own sphere, as for example the development of landed proprietorship out of purely military relations of subordination; but (2) the objective relation on which they founder has still a limited, primitive character and therefore *seems* personal, while,

in the modern world, personal relations flow purely out of relations of production and exchange (G, pp. 163-165; MEW, G, pp. 80-82).[3]

The extent to which the estranged elements of life were still controlled by man, at the expense of having exchange relations, allows Marx to conclude that feudal institutions provided certain guarantees of existence. For example, even serfs tended to own some land and were allowed a share in common lands (MEW, 23, pp. 743-745). Although coercion was a fact, under precapitalist social formations it tended to affect individuals quite differently than did the type of coercion encountered under capital:

> The bourgeoisie, wherever it has got the upper hand, has put an end to all feudal, patriarchal, idyllic relations. It has pitilessly torn asunder the motley feudal ties that bound man to his "natural superiors", and has left remaining no other nexus between man and man than naked self-interest, than callous "cash payment". It has drowned the most heavenly ecstasies of religious fervour, of chivalrous enthusiasm, of philistine sentimentalism, in the icy water of egotistical calculation. It has resolved personal worth into exchange value, and in place of the numberless indefeasible chartered freedoms, has set up that single, unconscionable freedom—Free Trade. In one word, for exploitation, veiled by religious and political illusions, it has substituted naked, shameless, direct, brutal exploitation (CW, 6, pp. 486-487; MEW, 4, pp. 464-465).

Thus far, the following has been established. On the one hand, individuals and their labor power were subject to an alien will even under precapitalist social formations. The product of labor, too, was only in part appropriated by the producers themselves. On the other hand, although the alien will appears to have been associated primarily with individuals, since the estranged life elements were still predominantly bound by man, impersonal, objective relations were also present. Marx's thesis that the division of labor has been an involuntary one ever since the emergence of private property, which itself is the result of estranged labor and exchange, is therefore not contradicted. For in precapitalist society, the producers could not organize all production on the basis of agreement, nor was exchange, which in itself causes division of labor, nonexistent.

DISCUSSION

Given the above assessment of the nature of precapitalist society, it must logically be concluded that, since Marx thought the division of labor was involuntary, individuals are estranged. This purely logical argument is not contradicted when we consider Marx's account of concrete life-situations under precapitalist social formations. Thus, it was possible to show how, according to Marx, individuals and their labor power are subject to an alien will. This subjection, as under capital, prevents man from living according to his nature, with the consequence that he is estranged. Man is estranged by virtue of the same evidence and reasoning Marx himself applied in his analysis of estrangement under capital. The conditions under which man is estranged may be different from those of capitalist production, but estrangement nevertheless exists. Man is not free as is the case under communism where estrangement is nonexistent (see also MEW, 26.3, p. 514; MEW, 4, p. 462).

Marx illustrated his theory of estrangement with examples from, and an analysis of, capitalist society. Therefore, in connection with precapitalist social formations, he only infrequently uses the term "estrangement" or "estranged." He does mention that under feudalism the earth is estranged from man and "confronts him in the shape of a few great lords." He also speaks of landed property as being "alienated (*entäussert*) man" and of precapitalist private property as being "man's actual externalisation (*Entäusserung*)" and "external to oneself (*Sich-äusserlichsein*)" (CW, 3, pp. 291-293; MEW, EB 1.T., pp. 531-532).[4] On the whole, however, there is little use of the vocabulary that accompanied Marx's early analysis of capitalist society. Of course, it must also be pointed out that most of Marx's efforts were not devoted to the analysis of precapitalist society but primarily to capitalist society, thus further influencing our judgment that he made only scant use of such terms as *Entfremdung* and *Entäusserung* in his analysis of precapitalist society. It would be a mistake, however, to conclude that Marx's theory of estrangement has no validity when it concerns precapitalist society. This theory should not be assessed on the basis of purely semantic criteria. Rather, vocabulary should merely be seen as a "tool" in conveying a particular theory, implying that to some extent at least a theory can be conveyed with different sets of vocabulary.

It follows that once the postulates of Marx's theory of estrangement—as he illustrates with reference to capitalist society—can clearly be defined and isolated, it is also possible to investigate whether the same postulates are being used in the analysis of precapitalist social formations. This is the way we proceeded in this work. First, the postulates of Marx's theory of estrangement, as he used it in his analysis of capitalist society, were identified. Then, in the first part of this chapter, it was found that Marx uses the same postulates when analyzing precapitalist social formations. The conclusion was drawn that, although the vocabulary Marx used seldom included the words "estrangement" and "alienation," man can still be said to be estranged even under precapitalist social formations (excluding primitive communistic societies). The major elements of Marx's theory of estrangement are not the words "estrangement" or "alienation" or derivatives thereof, but the notion of the involuntary division of labor. This notion also guides Marx's analysis of precapitalist social formations (see also MEW, 3, pp. 68-77).

IS MARX AN ANTI-INDUSTRIALIST ROMANTICIST?

Dawydow (1964: 50) maintains that Marx had a preconceived ideal of the "nature" of work and the "normal" relationship of the worker to his work according to which he analyzed work under capital. Marx did not hold such an ideal, however. This is not to say that he did not envision work as different under communism or that he did not admit that precapitalist and capitalist work differed. More important for Marx is the necessity that man be able to subject his labor power and its product to his own will and be able to live according to his nature. This necessity is the *sine qua non* of any society in which man is not estranged, regardless of the "nature" of work or the worker's relationship to it. In a society devoid of estrangement, man can be envisioned to have many dimensions. Such a vision of man may also be justified for communism. However, Marx never maintains that man in a society devoid of estrangement *must* be many-sided and that work *must* be of a certain nature. Neither estrangement nor nonestrangement is seen to depend on a definition of the ideal nature of work. It does, however, fully depend on whether one's labor power and product of labor are subject to an alien will. Following Dawydow's suggestion that Marx has a preconceived ideal of the nature of work when analyzing work under capital, Israel (1971:263) asserts that this ideal was influenced by the romanticist criticism of industrial society:

> The ideas concerning self-realization appear now to have been influenced by the existing conditions in preindustrialized, pre-capitalist society, being a part of the romanticist criticism of industrialized society. Among other things this criticism contained nostalgic, though probably not very realistic, views as to the work situation of the artisan, whose situation probably influenced Marx's ideal. The artisan could perhaps be seen as able to realize himself in his work activity.[5]

A closer look at the writings of Marx reveals that Israel's suggestion is not very convincing. It is, of course, true that Marx thought precapitalist society was less ruled than capitalist society by forces not controlled by man. He also admits that feudal society, for example, offered certain guarantees and degrees of freedom that were afterwards lost. It is also true that Marx believed that labor under the guild-corporation system was "still half artistic, half end-in-itself etc. Mastery," and that the capitalist was himself still a master-journeyman[6] (G, p. 497; MEW, G, p. 397):

> His position as master rests not only on his ownership of the conditions of production, but also on his own skill in the particular work. With the production of capital and from the very outset, the point is not this half-artistic relation to labour—which corresponds generally with the development of the use value of labour, the development of particular abilities of direct manual work, the formation of the human hand etc. The point from the outset is mass, because the point is exchange value and surplus value. The principle of developed capital is precisely to make special skill superfluous, and to make manual work directly physical labour, generally superfluous both as skill and as muscular exertion (G, p. 587; MEW, G, pp. 481-482).[7]

Even the guild-corporation system, which was not tied to the landholding class, made some material guarantees for the workers and human bonds that were lost under capital. "As journeyman (a genuine one) there is a certain communality in the consumption fund possessed by the master. While it is not the journeyman's *property* either, still, through the laws of the guild, tradition etc., at least co-possession etc." (G, p. 498; MEW, G, p. 397).

We may therefore conclude that precapitalist, preindustrial society offered conditions that in some ways were more dignifying than the wage slavery by which it was replaced. The estranged elements of life were still predominantly controlled by man rather than man being controlled by the forces of exchange which escaped the control of the participants. While Marx recognized these comparative differences, it would be a mistake to think he was idealizing preindustrial, precapitalist society.[8] For example, when discussing primitive accumulation, the early accumulation of capital, Marx suggests that it could occur only by transforming serfs and slaves into wage laborers and by means of "the expropriation of the immediate producers, i.e., the dissolution of private property based on the labour of its owner" (C1, p. 713). This means, of course, that the immediate producers also became wage laborers. Historically,

> private property of the labourer in his means of production is the foundation of petty industry, whether agricultural, manufacturing, or both; petty industry, again, is an essential condition for the development of social production and of the free individuality of the labourer himself. Of course, this petty mode of production exists also under slavery, serfdom, and other states of dependence. But it flourishes, it lets loose its whole energy, it attains its adequate classical form, only where the labourer is the private owner of his own means of labour set in action by himself: the peasant of the land which he cultivates, the artisan of the tool which he handles as a virtuoso (C1, p. 713; MEW, 23, p. 789).

Again, Marx alludes to the fact that the artisan's work was half artistic. However, he immediately points out the historical limits of this mode of production in both agriculture and industry:

> This mode of production pre-supposes parcelling of the soil, and scattering of the other means of production. As it excludes the concentration of these means of production, so it also excludes cooperation, division of labour within each seperate process of production, the control over, and the productive application of the forces

of Nature by society, and the free development of the social productive powers. It is compatible only with a system of production,
and a society, moving within narrow and more or less primitive bounds.
To perpetuate it would be, as Pecqueur rightly says, "to decree universal mediocrity." At a certain stage of development it brings forth
the material agencies for its own dissolution. From that moment new
forces and new passions spring up in the bosom of society; but the
old social organisation fetters them and keeps them down. It must
be annihilated; it is annihilated. Its annihilation, the transformation
of the individualised and scattered means of production into socially
concentrated ones, of the pigmy property of the many into the huge
property of the few. . . . Self-earned private property, that is based,
so to say on the fusing together of the isolated, independent labour-
ing-individual with the conditions of his labour, is supplanted by
capitalist private property, which rests on exploitation of the nominal-
ly free labour of others, i.e., on wage-labour (C1, pp. 713-714; MEW,
23, pp. 789-790).

Marx writes these words without any sign of regret for what was "lost"
as a result of the advance of the capitalist mode of production. In this
respect, he differs remarkably from the romanticists who mourn the old
social order disappearing in the face of rising capital.

In earlier stages of development the single individual seems to be
developed more fully, because he has not yet worked out his relationships in their fullness, or erected them as independent social powers
and relations opposite himself. It is as ridiculous to yearn for a return
to that original fullness as it is to believe that with this complete empti-
ness history has come to a standstill. The bourgeois viewpoint has never
advanced beyond this antithesis between itself and this romantic viewpoint, and therefore the latter will accompany it as legitimate antithesis
up to its blessed end (G, p. 162; MEW, G, p. 80).

In summary, Marx recognizes the differences between the capitalist and
precapitalist mode of production and the individual's fuller development
in precapitalist society. Even though for him work in precapitalist society
often assumes half-artistic proportions, he does not endorse it as an ideal

to be pursued or regained. There are two reasons for this. First, his ideal is communism, which is based on the development of the productive forces of man. Precapitalist production is little developed, however, and precludes further development. Thus, it effectively excludes itself as an example of production under communism as envisioned by Marx.[9] And since the precapitalist artisan with his half-artistic work cannot be separated from the mode of production in which he was active, he, too, is effectively excluded as an example of productive activity under communism. On this basis, Marx can say that it is ridiculous to yearn for a return to that original fullness of the individual at earlier stages of development. He would therefore agree with those who maintain that it is unrealistic to desire the reemergence of a society of artisans. However, those who hold such views often wrongly assert that Marx's view of the ideal society entails such an unrealistic desire.

That Marx cannot legitimately be criticized, as Israel does, for having been influenced by romanticist, unrealistic, and nostalgic criticism of industrialized society is evident through yet another example. In *The Poverty of Philosophy,* he criticizes Proudhon in the following way:

> M. Proudhon, not having understood even this one revolutionary side of the automatic workshop, takes a step backward and proposes to the worker that he make not only the twelfth part of a pin, but successively all twelve parts of it. The worker would thus come to know and realise the pin. This is M. Proudhon's synthetic labour. . . .
>
> To sum up, M. Proudhon has not gone further than the petty-bourgeois ideal. And to realise this ideal, he can think of nothing better than to take us back to the journeyman or, at most, to the master craftsman of the Middle Ages. It is enough, he says somewhere in his book, to have created a masterpiece once in one's life, to have felt oneself just once to be a man. Is not this, in form as in content, the masterpiece demanded by the craft guild of the Middle Ages (CW6, p. 190; MEW, 4, p. 157).[10]

Here we see that Marx's vision of the future does not exclude techniques of production that are generally associated with industrial society, the automatic factory being a case in point. In addition, Marx's observation that "the automatic workshop wipes out specialists and craft-idiocy" (CW6,

p. 190) and is revolutionary must be taken seriously. On the basis of a higher level of productivity, Marx foresees a new type of fullness of individual development, a fullness that is not modeled after that of earlier stages of development:

> What characterises the division of labour inside modern society is that it engenders specialities, specialists, and with them craft-idiocy. . . .
> What characterises the division of labour in the automatic workshop is that labour has there completely lost its specialised character. But the moment every special development stops, the need for universality, the tendency towards an integral development of the individual begins to be felt (CW6, p. 190; MEW, 4, p. 157).

Marx does not envision the ideal society as one in which labor productivity is low and in which the individual develops that type of fullness associated with the precapitalist artisan. Rather, he sees the productive power of man to be high, enabling the individual under communism to develop in ways hitherto unknown.

This brings us to the second reason why Marx does not endorse the quasi-artistic nature of the precapitalist mode of production as an ideal to be pursued. He does not picture communism as a society in which the means of production are split and held by many individuals, since "it is the association of individuals (assuming the advanced stage of modern productive forces, of course) which puts the conditions of the free development and movement of individuals under their control" (CW5, p. 80; MEW, 3, p. 75). Yet, precapitalist production was based on the fact that many owned the means of production necessary to maintain themselves through their individual and isolated labor (*Selbstbetätigung,* or self-activity). Marx calls this type of activity "one-sided" (CW5, p. 82), and he maintains that "although isolated labour (its material conditions presupposed) can also create use values, it can create neither wealth nor culture" (CGP, p. 5; MEW, 19, p. 17).

Again, Marx hands down a strong indictment of the type of work found in precapitalist, preindustrial society. But there is another basis for the rejection of this type of work which relates to Marx's notion of the development of the individual. This development is still incomplete in precapitalist societies. (See also the discussion on the development of the individual in chapter 7.) Although the artisans owned the means for their self-activity, "they themselves remained subordinate to the division of labour and their own instrument of production" (CW5, p. 88; MEW, 3, p. 68). Under communism, however, man will no longer be subject to the involuntary division of labor, thus enabling "the development of a totality of capacities" (CW5, p. 87; MEW, 3, p. 68).

These two factors then—lack of productivity and the concomitant lack of development of the individual in precapitalist society—show why Marx is not an anti-industrial romanticist. Communist society, after capital has "laid the appropriate foundations," is seen as the only society in which the fullest possible development of the individual can occur. This development cannot be understood to mean that individuals will become latter-day artisans, since the mode of production will vary greatly from that of precapitalist societies. However, this in itself does not preclude that individuals will not also be artists.

NOTES

1. For Marx, "estranged labour is the direct cause of private property" (CW, 3, p. 280; MEW, EB 1.T., p. 521). This does not contradict his postulate that the involuntary division of labor and private property occurred simultaneously, since the immediate consequence of the appropriation of the labor power of others by some is private property.

2. Similarly in MEW, G, p. 81.

3. It could be said that Marx contradicts himself in *Capital*. There he says that, since personal dependence characterizes the social relations of production in the Middle Ages and

> personal dependence forms the ground-work of society, there is no necessity for labour and its products to assume a fantastic form different from their reality. They take the shape, in the transactions of society, of services in kind and payments in kind. Here the particular and natural form of labour, and not, as in a society based on production of commodities, its general abstract form is the immediate social form of labour (C1, pp. 81-82; MEW, 23, p. 91).

While he admits in the *Grundrisse* that objective relations exist under the feudal order, the above statement could be considered contradictory. A closer look at another passage in *Capital* may resolve this apparent contradiction:

> [F]rom the moment there is a free sale, by the labourer himself, of labour-power as a commodity . . . that commodity production is generalised and becomes the typical form of production . . . . Only when and where wage-labour is its basis does commodity production impose itself upon society as a whole. (C1, pp. 550-551; MEW, 23, p. 613).

Hence, commodity production did exist under feudalism, which in itself could represent one form of objective relations in addition to military subordination. Rather, the commodity production remains limited as long as personal dependence persists. The matter is one of emphasis.

4. In the *Manuscripts,* Marx writes that "all human activity hitherto has been labour—that is, industry—activity estranged from itself" (CW, 3, p. 303; MEW, EB 1.T., pp. 542-543).

Commenting on the economic theory of the Physiocrats, Marx points out that *"Physiocracy* represents directly the decomposition of feudal property in *eco*-nomic terms, but it therefore just as directly represents its *economic metamorphosis* and restoration, save that now its language is no longer feudal but economic." However, with the Physiocrats "labour is not yet grasped in its generality and abstraction: it is still bound to a particular *natural element as its matter,* and it is therefore only recognised in a *particular mode of existence determined by nature.* It is therefore still only a specific, *particular* alienation of man." (CW, 3, p. 292; MEW, EB 1.T., pp. 531-532).

5. Israel seems to have superimposed the notion of self-realization on the thought of Marx. To my knowledge, Marx does not use a notion of self-realization to analyze the worker's situation. If this notion has any place in Marx's thought, it is in conjunction with the notion that man should be able to subject his labor power to his *own* will and to appropriate the product of his labor. It is inappropriate, however, for Israel to view self-realization as a negative function of industrial society and as a positive function of preindustrial society. It would be equally inappropriate to view the notion of self-realization in psychological terms. Should one want to define self-realization in terms of labor as a manifestation and development of human capacities, Marx would reply by saying: "How could labour ever be *anything but* a 'manifestation of human capacities'?" (CW, 5, p. 482; MEW, 3, p. 471).

6. "Capitalist himself still master-journeyman" (G, p. 497). Here the word "capitalist" is used in the figurative sense, indicating that the master does own the consumption fund, a great part, if not all, of the means of production (see also MEW, G, p. 397), and does extract a surplus from his workers. However, neither wage labor nor exchange has yet developed fully. Capital is therefore not truly capital and the master is not a capitalist as Marx generally uses the term.

7. At another place in the *Grundrisse,* Marx states:

> For example, in guild and craft labour, where capital itself still has a limited form, and is still entirely immersed in a particular substance, hence is not yet *capital as such,* labour, too, appears as still immersed in its particular specificity: not in the totality and abstraction of labour *as such,* in which it confronts capital. That is to say that labour is of course in each single case a specific labour, but capital can come into relation with every *specific* labour (G, pp. 296-297; MEW, G, p. 204).

8. This is just as much a mistake as it would be to label Marx a mere trade unionist on the basis that he supports the attempts of workers to obtain a higher wage at the expense of the capitalists' profit (WPP, pp. 77-78; MEW, 16, pp. 151-152).

9. Only through capital, at the expense of the laborer's private ownership of his means of production, does further development occur.

10. Referring to the modern farmer, the capitalist and the worker, he asserts that

> they feel an attachment only for the price of their production, the monetary product. Hence the jeremiads of the reactionary parties, who offer up all their prayers for the return of feudalism, of the good old patriarchal life, of the simple manners and the virtues of our forefathers. The subjection of the soil to the laws which dominate all other industries is and always will be the subject of interested condolences (CW6, p. 202; MEW, 4, p. 170).

Note that Marx calls those who envision or call for a return of the precapitalist mode of production reactionaries. Thus, he politically rejects those values which some claim are present in his thought. A similar rejection occurs in the *Manifesto* when petty-bourgeois socialism is being discussed:

> In its positive aims, however, this form of socialism aspires either to restoring the old means of production and of exchange, and with them the old property relations, and the old society, or to cramping the modern means of production and of exchange, within the framework of the old property relations that have been, and were bound to be, exploded by those means. In either case, it is both reactionary and Utopian (CW6, pp. 509-510; MEW, 4, p. 485).

9

The Scope and Applicability
of Marx's Theory of Estrangement

Before anything can be said about the scope and applicability of Marx's theory of estrangement, we must clarify whether it is legitimate to speak of only *one* theory of estrangement. If it is not legitimate to speak of only one theory, it will have to be specified which theory of estrangement is referred to when addressing the applicability of Marx's theory of estrangement.

Some students of Marx maintain that he abandoned the terms "estrangement" and "alienation" in his later work, and based on this assertion, they argue that Marx also abandoned or changed his theory of estrangement. This argument is weak on at least two counts. First, the content of a theory should not, and cannot, be evaluated solely on the basis of whether a certain vocabulary is present. Thus, by investigating the properties of Marx's theory of estrangement in the foregoing analysis, it was possible to show that these properties do not change, although the vocabulary may undergo some changes. It was shown that Marx's theory of estrangement is derived from his definition of human nature, a definition that is present in both his early and later work. Man is said to be estranged if, contrary to his nature, he is prevented from subjecting his labor power, as well as the product of his labor, to his own will. If one is so prevented, the existence of an involuntary division of labor can be implied. If, therefore, it can be shown that

Marx, throughout his work, maintained the same definition of human nature as well as his search for a society with a voluntary division of labor, it can be concluded that his theory of estrangement remained the same throughout his work, regardless of any changes in his vocabulary from the early to the later writings. As shown above, Marx adhered to an unaltered definition of human nature, and the notion of an involuntary division of labor is absolutely central to his theory of estrangement. Throughout his work, he viewed the desirable society as one with a voluntary division of labor and, therefore, free from estrangement. As a consequence, we can conclude that Marx's theory of estrangement remained the same.

Second, those who maintain that Marx abandoned or changed his theory of estrangement on the basis that he abandoned the terms "alienation" and "estrangement," are at least partially incorrect in their assertions. In an excellent treatment of the subject, Mészáros (1972) shows that in many instances Marx continued to use the above terms in his later works and did not abandon them at all.[1] As can be seen from the quotes given so far, this study confirms Mészáros' assessment. Marx did, indeed make use of the terms in his later writings, though not as frequently as in his *Manuscripts*, and his theory of estrangement remains unchanged throughout his works since the theory's properties were never abandoned or altered.

Israel (1971, 1976) suggests that Marx abandoned his theory of estrangement for a theory of reification. He bases this argument on the assertion that Marx changed his theory of human nature. Before the *Theses on Feuerbach*, Israel claims, Marx adhered to a philosophical anthropological position which claims

> a general abstract human nature which contrasts with the idea that human nature is a historically determined product that changed as societal conditions change. In the sixth of his "Theses on Feuerbach" Marx explicitly rejects this anthropological position by asserting that man's nature *is* the totality of his societal relations. By doing so he also removed one of the essential preconditions for his theory of alienation. It was abandoned, but reappeared in a new form as the theory of reification (Israel, 1976:47).[2]

Israel's position, shared by LeoGrande, (1977) is fundamentally incorrect, however. While Marx undisputably took Feuerbach to task for not seeing man in an historical light, his theory of estrangement was never based on a theory of human nature that did not take history into account. Rather, as shown in Chapter 2, this theory was derived from a biological definition of human nature. This definition is not subject to the historical relativism argument, an argument with which Marx not only criticizes Feuerbach's understanding of human nature but also Bentham's and others'. The biological definition is empirically arrived at by comparing man with animals. This becomes in the thought of Marx "human nature in general," while those aspects of human nature that are subject to historical change signify "human nature as modified in each historical period." As pointed out earlier in a different context, Israel does not note this very important distinction. Thus, he reaches some wrong conclusions concerning Marx's adherence to his theory of estrangement as formulated in the *Manuscripts.* That Israel does not appreciate this distinction fully can be observed in the following passage which, consequently, is very unclear. Israel says that Marx differentiates between "(1) 'human nature at a given historical period' being a consequence of man's existing social relations and (2) man's 'general human nature as it is changed in the historical process', though always being a consequence of the social relations he has created himself" (Israel 1971:57).[3]

Israel's and LeoGrande's thesis presents some additional problems. First, as shown in Chapter 2, those who argue that Marx did not conceive human nature to be socially conditioned until he wrote the *Theses on Feuerbach* are factually incorrect.[4] Second, it is not meaningful to argue that Marx abandoned his early theory of estrangement in favor of a theory of reification, since even his early and only theory of estrangement is a theory of reification. The present study shows abundant evidence[5] that in his early work Marx already perceived man under capital to be dominated by an alien will and alien forces, by the products of his own labor. Precisely this element of reification has always distinguished Marx's concept of estrangement from Hegel's, in which estrangement is seen to result from the mere objectification of labor.[6] We do not argue here that Marx paid the same attention to the processes of reification in his *Manuscripts* as he did in his later works starting with the *German Ideology.* However, a distinction between his theory of estrangement and his theory of reification is not only arbitrary but also unjustified. The differential attention he paid to processes of reification is quite a different matter, since Marx's theory of estrangement is categorically also a theory of reification. Man is estranged because both his labor power and the product of his labor are subject to an alien will, that is, because man is subject to an involuntary division of labor, a division that he controls neither at his place of work nor in the society at large. Under communism, this would not be so and estrangement would be abolished.

THE QUESTION OF BEING MORE OR LESS ESTRANGED

The secondary literature dealing with Marx's theory of estrangement often asserts that estrangement can have different magnitudes. That is, Marx's theory of estrangement is viewed in such a way that estrangement as such is seen to exist to a greater or lesser extent.[7] For example, Ollman (1976:132, 245-246, 252, 308) generally speaks of degrees of estrangement, as does Mészáros (1972:249) and Petrović (1967:149-150), while Mandel and Novack (1973:43) and Mészáros (1972:249) speak of progressive de-estrangement, or a decreasing trend of estrangement. Archibald (1976:69-70) speaks of differences of estrangement among classes, "between capitalist and non-capitalist societies" and between "currently capitalist societies and their own histories."

According to Marx, all estrangement is essentially reducible to the fact that man is subject to an alien will, that is, an involuntary division of labor. Moreover, man under precapitalist social formations can also be said to be estranged as long as the division of labor can be shown to be an involuntary one. Whether it be the involuntary division of labor under feudalism or capitalism, estrangement remains estrangement. Estrangement, which for Marx is the byproduct of any involuntary division of labor, is therefore a qualitative and not a quantitative phenomenon. If Marx is not to be misinterpreted, estrangement must be viewed as a dichotomous phenomenon. It exists wherever man is prevented from living according to his nature, as a result of the subjection of his labor power and the product of his labor to an alien will. It ceases to exist under communism where man is free from the domination of other men and where the division of labor is therefore a voluntary one. Marx's concept of estrangement cannot therefore be interpreted as a phenomenon of different magnitudes. Man either is or is not estranged; estrangement either exists or it does not exist. This position is the direct logical consequence of Marx's theory of estrangement as interpreted here. If it is correct, then no evidence to the contrary should be found in the writings of Marx, and indeed, this seems to be the case.

Marx does, of course, mention that the alien forces that control man have become more powerful, and increasingly so, ever since the emergence of private property and the involuntary division of labor.

> In the present epoch, the domination of material relations over individuals, and the suppression of individuality by fortuitous circumstances, has assumed its sharpest and most universal form, thereby setting existing individuals a very definite task. It has set them the task of replacing the domination of circumstances and of chance over individuals by the domination of individuals over chance and circumstances. . . . This task, dictated by present-day relations, coincides with the task of organising society in a communist way (CW5, p. 438; MEW, 3, p. 424).

In the *Holy Family*, he writes:

> All communist and socialist writers proceeded from the observation that . . . all *progress of the Spirit* had so far been *progress against the mass of mankind,* driving it into an ever more dehumanised situation. They therefore declared *"progress"* (see *Fourier*) to be an inadequate, abstract *phrase;* they assumed (see *Owen* among others) a fundamental flaw in the civilized world (CW, 4, p. 84; MEW, 2, p. 88; see also MEW, EB 1.T., p. 543).

When Marx says that the alien forces that control man are becoming more and more powerful, he is referring to the consequences of estrangement and not of estrangement as such. While the consequences of estrangement can be viewed as more or less severe (that is, they can be viewed in terms of magnitude), this is quite different from viewing estrangement as such in terms of a magnitude. Even when Marx uses the term "estrangement" (*Entfremdung*) in this context, it designates the alien force that increasingly dominates man in the form of the objective conditions of production, that is, capital. The conversion of surplus labor into capital or accumulation "reveals that . . . unpaid labour of the worker confronts his as the *totality of the objective conditions of labour.* In this form it confronts him as an alien property with the result that the capital which is antecedent to his labour, appears to be independent of it" (TS3, p. 352;

MEW, 26.3, p. 344). At another place, the same theme is further elaborated in the following way:

> With the advance in the productivity of social labour, accompanied as it is by the growth of constant capital, a relatively ever increasing part of the annual product of labour will, therefore, fall to the share of capital as such, and thus property in the form of capital (apart from revenue) will be constantly increasing and proportionately that part of value which the individual worker and even the working class creates, will be steadily decreasing, compared with the product of their past labour that confronts them as capital. The alienation and the antagonism between labour-power and the objective conditions of labour which have become independent in the form of capital, thereby grow continuously (TS2, p. 416; MEW, 26.2, pp. 417-418).[8]

Clearly, in the context in which the term *Entfremdung* is used here, it does not designate categoric estrangement, that is, that man is estranged because his labor power and the product of his labor are subject to an alien will. Rather, it signifies that, given categoric estrangement, the consequences thereof become more and more overpowering. The alien property confronting the worker is increasingly powerful. The categorically estranged product of man's labor confronts him in ever more "estranging" ways, being ever more drastic to his existence and survival as a human being. During feudalism, the estranged elements of life tended to be bound by man (see Chapter 8), thus producing conditions that were often more dignifying. This is not the case under capital. In both cases, however, man is estranged because of his subjection to an involuntary division of labor.

It must therefore be concluded that Marx clearly distinguishes between estrangement as such and the consequences of estrangement. The consequences of estrangement do not reflect on the magnitude of estrangement as such, inasmuch as estrangement as such is a qualitative and not a quantitative phenomenon. Indeed, the Marxian system of thought allows for only a separation between estrangement as such and the consequences of estrangement. It can be shown in many ways that a distinction must be made between the two if Marx's theory of estrangement is not to be violated. Several of these ways will be discussed here.

If estrangement were thought to have a magnitude, it would logically have to be concluded that man's estrangement is greater or less because his subjection to an alien will is greater or less. As can immediately be seen, however, this is an absurd conclusion inasmuch as an alien will remains an alien will, for "alien will" or "involuntary division of labor" are qualitiative and not quantitative phenomena.

The objection may be made that subjection to an alien will may occur only part of the time, or for some people not at all. Hence, it could be maintained that under feudalism, the serf was forced to work the land of the lord only during some days of the week, while on the other days of the week he was allowed to care for his own subsistence by working his own land. In addition, the example of the capitalist may be given, who is forced neither to sell his labor power nor to produce a product that could become subject to an alien will. The answer to this objection lies first in the recognition that Marx himself does not distinguish between the estrangement of the capitalist and that of the worker in quantitative terms. He believes they are both estranged, although he considers the consequences of the capitalist's estrangement to be different from those of the worker.[9] For the capitalist, estrangement at least has consequences that entail the "semblance of a human existence."

The capitalist is also subject to the involuntary division of labor. As has already been pointed out, he is merely the human agent of capital, and as a human being he is subject to forces that he does not control. An example of this control is competition which regulates the capitalist's activities in terms of investment and exchange of products. In fact, his class status as a capitalist designates his involvement in an involuntary division of labor.[10]

From the vantage point of Marx's theory of the development of the individual, the capitalist cannot develop freely and fully, even if he manages to live in luxury. Marx's pronouncement on the Roman nobility may be applied in this context. Although in ancient Rome "the individuals may appear great, . . . "there can be no conception here of a free and full development either of the individual or of the society, since such development stands in contradiction to the original relation" (see chapter 7, footnote 8). As a consequence, unless all are free from domination of man by man, the development of individuals remains limited even for those whose life has "the semblance of a human existence." We therefore agree with Ollman (1976:156) when he says that the capitalist's estrangement also "stands out not only in all he is but in all he is not. Communist fulfillment is equally unavailable to both classes." This relates to our discussion of the estrangement from the species and from man. Since the interaction among human beings in situations where man dominates man is not in accord with the nature of the species, man is said to be estranged from the species and from one another. Although the capitalist, like the Roman, may have abundant time and resources, his individual development remains stunted. The reason is that he is not interacting with others according to the natural ability of the species, that is, in such a way that the "need on the part of one can be satisfied by the product of the other." (See also Chapter 2.)

From various points of view, then, Marx's concept of estrangement cannot be viewed as a quantity rather than as a quality. Estrangement as such, which is a qualitative phenomenon, must be strictly distinguished from the consequences of estrangement, which is a quantitative phenomenon. Students of Marx have too often failed to make this important distinction. As a result, even if unknowingly, Marx is interpreted from a reformist perspective. Regardless of the consequences of estrangement, the only society Marx advocated was one free from estrangement—free from any domination of man by man. It is therefore impossible to measure estrangement without misinterpreting Marx in the process. Consequently, Archibald's (1976:69-70) suggestion that we measure what Marx called estrangement, in order to determine differences in estrangement among classes and societies, is very misleading.

Seeman bases his rationale for his work on estrangement on the same misleading attempt to measure what Marx calls estrangement. Seeman says that his work represents an attempt to "make more organized sense of one of the great traditions in sociological thought; and to make the traditional interest in alienation more amenable to sharp empirical statement" (Seeman, 1959:511). He reiterates this rationale in his paper "The Urban Alienation: Some Dubious Theses from Marx to Marcuse":

> To speak of dubious theses about alienation is to suggest an interest in secularizing this more or less "sacred" concept; it is to suggest that there is something here about which an empirical demonstration has to be made—the critical, evocative, and even romantic spirit that has infused the literature on alienation, whatever its very valid uses in some respects, being no substitute for clarity and rigor (Seeman, 1971a:135).

As well intentioned as Seeman's position may be, it misses the point. What Marx called estrangement is in need neither of "clarity and rigor," nor of a "sharp empirical" statement of the kind Seeman intends to provide. It can simply not be measured, although Marx himself derived what he called estrangement empirically. Admittedly, the empirical categories Marx used are of a different empirical order than those Seeman has in mind. Nevertheless, they are empirical categories. By investigating the differences between man and animal, Marx determines what he calls human nature in general. As a result of being subject to an involuntary division of labor, however, man is prevented from living according to his nature and is estranged. Marx's notion of estrangement is a straightforward, logical procedure based on empirical data. Thus, man is estranged as long as his labor power and the product of his labor are subject to an alien will. However—and this point Seeman and others fail to recognize—the subjection to an alien will is an occurrence of a dichotomous kind; the subjection either exists or it does not exist, and it is therefore not measurable in terms of quantitities.

WHAT MARX CALLS ESTRANGEMENT: A CAUSE OF CERTAIN IDENTIFIABLE BEHAVIOR OR ATTITUDES?

Students of Marx in various disciplines have been mistaken not only in their attempt to measure estrangement, but also in viewing estrangement *as such* as the cause of certain identifiable behavior or attitudes. This is true of those who are concerned with operationalizing and measuring estrangement as well as of Schaff (1970a: 107, 135, 223, 225, 227), who implies that estrangement leads to "the arms race," "nationalism," "racial hatred," "religious intolerance," "certain forms of family organization," "depersonalization," "impoverishment of human personality," and "discrepancies in artistic tastes and opinions." Israel (1971: 83-84) makes similar inferences. He postulates that if individuals are unable to live according to their human nature, as Marx understands it, they will experience estrangement. To assume that individuals can experience their estrangement presupposes that individuals can make causal inferences as to which feelings are caused by what Marx calls estrangement and which feelings are caused by something else. The emphasis here is not on whether the feelings can be identified perfectly. Rather, it is on the implicit or explicit assumption, which students of Marx often hold, that Marx's theory of estrangement lends itself to making causal inferences. According to this assumption, it is postulated, for example, that estrangement causes certain identifiable feelings or "discrepancies in artistic tastes and opinions."[11] The interpretation of Marx's theory of estrangement given in this study, however, shows this view to be incorrect.

The reasons why behavior, feelings, or attitudes cannot meaningfully be said to be caused by estrangement lie in the lack of variance. Thus, nothing is known about the state of nonestrangement (true communism). Neither is estrangement under feudalism or capitalism seen to exist in greater or lesser quantities; rather, Marx views it as a dichotomous phenomenon. As a result, variance can not be obtained from historical comparisons. The same holds true for inter or intrasocietal comparisons, since there as well estrangement does not lend itself to measurement.

Hence, man is estranged, because he is subject to an involuntary division of labor, but it is impossible to determine how estrangement causes certain identifiable behavior, feelings, or attitudes. Theoretically, such a determination could be made only if it was possible to observe behavior, feelings, or attitudes under conditions of nonestrangement or various degrees of estrangement. Therefore, any hypothesis or claim implying that estrangement, as defined by Marx, is the cause of certain identifiable kinds of behavior, feelings, or attitudes in the present society must be termed speculative and cannot be verified empirically because of a lack of variance.[12] Of course, we maintain that what Marx calls estrangement is not manifest in certain types of behavior, attitudes, or feelings; this would clearly be an untenable position. According to Marx's theory of estrangement, it is impossible to identify which particular behavior, attitudes, or feelings are caused by the fact that man is estranged and therefore would not exist under nonestrangement. Israel and Schaff are not the only scholars who point to estrangement as the cause of certain identifiable behavior, feelings, or attitudes. Others (Strmiska, 1974:112 and Rousset, 1974:251, for example) are also mistaken on this point, although some, for example, Israel (1971) and Gabel, et al. (1974) are very critical of previous attempts to measure estrangement.

Numerous social scientists whose intention it is to measure estrangement also view estrangement as a cause and often theoretically link their enterprise with Marx's theory of estrangement (Dean, 1961; Barakat, 1969; Seeman, 1959, 1971a, 1971b). With the help of some theoretical reasoning, estrangement is seen to cause particular and identifiable social or psychological phenomena which then serve as indicators or dimensions of estrangement. Social scientists postulate that, when measured, these indicators or dimensions will directly reflect the degree and nature of estrangement. As we already pointed out in this chapter, estrangement cannot be measured if Marx is not to be misinterpreted. What is of particular interest right now, however, is the widespread notion that estrangement can be seen to cause identifiable behavior, feelings, or attitudes, and how this notion manifests itself with those social scientists whose attempt it is to measure estrangement.

Seeman has pioneered in the attempt to measure estrangement, and many have followed in his footsteps (Fischer, 1973; Neal and Rettig, 1967; Dean, 1961; and Middleton, 1963).[13] Seeman (1972a: 387) assumes that estrangement causes identifiable and particular feelings or attitudes. He defines his measures as follows:

1. Powerlessness—There is not much that I can do about most of the important problems that we face today.
2. Meaninglessness—Things have become so complicated in the world today that I really don't understand just what is going on.
3. Normlessness—In order to get ahead in the world today, you are almost forced to do some things which are not right.
4. Cultural estrangement—I am not much interested in the TV programs, movies, and magazines that most people seem to like.
5. Social isolation—I often feel lonely.
6. Self-estrangement in work—I really don't enjoy most of the work that I do, but I feel that I must do it in order to have other things that I need and want.

If the subject who is confronted with these measures discovers in her/himself the same feelings or perceives his surroundings in the same way, he is said to be estranged. Thus, estrangement as Marx understands it is postulated to cause identifiable and particular feelings which in turn, if measured, are seen to confirm the existence of estrangement.

Did Marx himself believe that particular and identifiable attitudes or feelings resulted from what he called estrangement? For this answer, our analysis will focus on certain passages in his early work.

It has been shown (Wallimann, 1975:280) that translations of a particular passage from Marx wrongly imply that he saw estrangement as the cause of certain feelings, attitudes, or behavior. These misleading translations appear at least in Tucker (1972:105) and Israel (1971:52).[14] Tucker's text says that the propertied class *"experiences the alienation* as a sign of its own power," while Israel's states that the proletariat "feels itself crushed *by* this self-alienation" (emphasis mine). In both instances, estrangement is postulated to generate certain identifiable feelings or experiences, while in fact Marx did not imply this at all:

> [T]he propertied class and the proletariat present the same human self-estrangement. But the former class feels at ease and strengthened in this self-estrangement, it recognises estrangement as *its own power* and has the *semblance* of a human existence. The latter feels annihilated in estrangement; it sees in it its own powerlessness and the reality of an inhuman existence (CW, 2, p. 36; MEW, 2, p. 37).[15]

The consequences of estrangement, as the above passage indicates, differ according to one's social position and in ways that can be contradictory. Thus, the propertied class feels at ease and strengthened, while the proletariat feels annihilated in its estrangement.[16] Under these circumstances, it would not make any sense to postulate, for example, that estrangement causes a feeling of annihilation, since it could equally be maintained that estrangement also causes the opposite feeling. Yet, Seeman proceeds on the assumption that estrangement causes specific and identifiable feelings or attitudes. If these feelings or attitudes can be found to be present in individuals, estrangement is considered to be present. According to our interpretation, however, estrangement is not defined by the feelings or attitudes it causes, but by the fact that man is subject to an involuntary division of labor and is unable to live according to his nature.

In this context, the following passage must also be considered:

> What, then, constitutes the alienation of labour? First, the fact that labour is *external* to the worker, i.e., it does not belong to his intrinsic nature; that in his work, therefore, he does not affirm himself but denies himself, does not feel content but unhappy, does not develop freely his physical and mental energy but mortifies his body and ruins his mind. The worker therefore only feels himself outside his work, and in his work feels outside himself. He feels at home

when he is not working, and when he is working he does not feel at home. His labour is therefore not voluntary, but coerced; it is *forced labour* (CW, 3, p. 274; MEW, EB 1.T., p. 514).[17]

It would be wrong to conclude from this quotation that Marx saw certain feelings or attitudes result from estrangement, and that estrangement can be identified with such feelings or attitudes. Rather, this passage must be interpreted within a framework that distinguishes estrangement as such from its consequences. Since the worker is forced to sell his labor power "labor is *external* to the worker"; it is "forced labour." Hence the worker is estranged. In very general terms, his and the estrangement of all other individuals allows for a world which they do not fully control, which they do not fully subject to their own will. It allows for a world in which, un-like under communism, man is dominated and subject to an involuntary division of labor affecting all. However, not all are equally affected. For example, the workers are forced to sell their labor power. The capitalist, although subject to an involuntary division of labor and therefore estranged, is not compelled to sell his labor power. As a result, he is not subject to many of the consequences brought about by circumstances he does not control. For the worker, the world he does not control has quite different consequences. For him, it means that work is external to him, that he feels unhappy, and so forth.

The existence of estrangement in general (that is, the existence of *any* involuntary division of labor) allows for the emergence of societal structures and processes that are not under the conscious control of societal members and that have had different consequences in different historical epochs. These consequences may be perceived as "burdensome,"[18] although estrange-ment remains a constant in view of the persistence of an involuntary divi-sion of labor.

Here I disagree with Ollman (1976:132) who fails to make a clear dis-tinction between estrangement as such and its various consequences. He maintains that the "forms of alienation differ for each class because their position and style of life differ, and, as expected, the proletariat's affliction is the most severe." On the contrary, estrangement is a con-stant since all are subject to an involuntary division of labor and are pre-vented from living according to their nature. According to our opinion, only the consequences of estrangement vary. However, this is not the same as saying that the forms of estrangement vary.

Within any particular historical period, these societal structures and processes can also be seen to have agreeable consequences. Although both the capitalists and the workers are estranged, being subject to an involuntary division of labor, the processes that arose because of estrangement affect both classes quite differently.

It is therefore meaningful to speak of estrangement as that condition which brings about a social world that escapes full control by the participants. It is meaningless to view estrangement as a cause of particular, identifiable feelings, behavior, and attitudes. First, such a cause cannot be verified because of a lack of variance and, second, such feelings, behavior, and attitudes can never be identified as the only ones resulting from estrangement. Third, Marx himself did not view estrangement as the cause of only a select number of identifiable feelings, attitudes, and behaviors. Any attempt to do so would imply that estrangement constitutes only certain phenomena perceived to be undesirable or arbitrarily selected by the social scientist.

ESTRANGEMENT AS AN OBJECTIVELY DEFINED CONCEPT

It is frequently debated whether Marx's concept of estrangement should be defined according to objective or subjective criteria. (See, for example, Israel, 1971; Schacht, 1971; and Fischer, 1976.) Subjective criteria are seen to involve "a state of mind," while a definition based on objective criteria "involves a condition of the whole or parts of society" (Mizruchi, 1964:46).

Based on our interpretation of Marx's theory of estrangement, it can be concluded that Marx defines estrangement according to objective criteria: individuals are estranged because they are subject to an involuntary division of labor, and not because they exhibit a certain "state of mind." The rather fruitless debate on whether estrangement is objectively or subjectively defined is partially attributable to the fact that students of Marx have not separated estrangement as such from the consequences of estrangement. Thus, many have mistaken particular consequences for the elements defining estrangement. Seeman's social-psychological operationalizations are a case in point. However, as has already been established, estrangement cannot be defined on the basis of certain manifestations, since the manifestations vary from one historical epoch to another as well as in a given population at a given time. Accordingly, once a separation is made between estrangement as such and the consequences of estrangement, it immediately becomes obvious that estrangement cannot be defined on the basis of a "state of mind" which individuals exhibit, since any such "state of mind" must be seen as a consequence of estrangement.

NOTES

1. For details, the reader is advised to consult Meszaros' study (1972:217-27) directly.

2. Apparently, without knowing of Israel's work (see Israel, 1976 and 1971), LeoGrande (1977) advances the same thesis concerning Marx's departure from his theory of estrangement outlined in the *Manuscripts.*

3. It may also be pointed out that neither Meszaros (1972:148, 163, 170) nor Ollman (1976:74, 80-81, 85, 92, 110) makes a well-defined distinction between the two definitions of human nature in Marx.

4. See also Chapter 2, note 2. In the *Manuscripts,* Marx says that Feuerbach's great achievement is "the establishment of *true materialism* and of *real science,* by making the social relationship of 'man to man' the basic principle of the theory." And in a letter to Feuerbach in August 1844, Marx wrote:

> In these writings you have—whether intentionally I do not know—given a philosophical basis to socialism, and the communists, too, have similarly understood these works in that sense. The unity of man with man based on the real differences between men, the concept of human species transferred from the heaven of abstraction to the real earth, what is this other than the concept of society! (McLellan, 1971:184).

Marx had apparently revised his appraisal of Feuerbach by the time he wrote the *Theses on Feuerbach;* nevertheless, his concept of man was one of social man. Yet, Israel writes that "in the sixth of his 'Theses on Feuerbach' Marx explicitly rejects this anthropological position by asserting that man's nature *is* the totality of his social relations" (Israel, 1976:47).

5. See also Chapter 2, pp. 62-71.

6. Similarly, Lukacs' identification of estrangement with objectification in his *History and Class Consciousness* may be mentioned. However, Lukacs retreated from this position later in his life by admitting that the interpretation in this book was too Hegelian (Lukacs, 1970:25).

7. Since no distinction is usually made between Marx's use of the terms "estrangement" and "alienation," students of Marx speak of alienation as existing to a greater or lesser extent, referring to what is here called estrangement as existing to a greater or lesser extent.

8. *Entfremdung* (estrangement) is used by Marx. As already indicated *Entfremdung* should be translated estrangement, and not alienation.

9. See chapter 2, pp. 37-38.

10. As earlier, "division of labor" also includes the division of labor in society as a whole.

11. "Cause" is used here to designate even the mere association of specific behavior, feelings, or attitudes with estrangement.

12. It is indeed ironical that, according to this analysis, those social scientists may be said to be speculative who, according to their own intentions, wish to avoid specu ative statements. In this context, Seeman's (1971a:135) passage cited above may be recalled.

13. It is impossible to address and critically deal with all the literature that has been built up around the attempt to measure estrangement. Seeman is therefore selected here as a representative example of a whole group of scholars.

14. The translation of the same passage in the *Collected Works*, which appeared after my paper (Wallimann, 1975) was in press, avoids the same mistakes.

15. Note also that "estrangement" rather than "alienation" is correctly used here to translate *Entfremdung*.

16. Similarly, the consequences of estrangement are distinguished from estrangement as such (that is, from the inability to subject one's labor power and product of labor to one's own will) in other passages:

. . . the more objects the worker produces the less he can possess and the more he falls under the sway of his product, capital.

All these consequences are implied in the statement that the worker is related to the *product of his labour* as to an *alien* object (CW, 3, p. 272; MEW, EB 1.T., p. 512).

(According to the economic laws the estrangement of the worker in his object is expressed thus: the more the worker produces, the less he has to consume; the more values he creates, the more valueless, the more unworthy he becomes; the better formed his product, the more deformed becomes the worker; the more civilised his object, the more barbarous becomes the worker; the more powerful labour becomes, the more powerless becomes the worker; the more ingenious labour becomes, the less ingenious becomes the worker and the more he becomes nature's servant.) (CW, 3, p. 273; MEW, EB 1.T., p. 513).

This estrangement manifests itself in part in that the sophistication of needs and of the means [of their satisfaction] on the one side produces a bestial barbarism, a complete, crude, abstract simplicity of need, on the other; or rather in that it merely reproduces itself in its opposite (CW, 3, p. 307; MEW, EB 1.T., p. 548).

While these statements share the distinction between estrangement and its consequences, they also show that the consequences of estrangement differ. The consequences simultaneously represent wealth and poverty, refinement and barbarity, sophistication and crude simplicity. In sum, the consequences of estrangement entail contradictions.

17. Note that Marx talks in the above quote of "alienation" (*Entäusserung*) and not of "estrangement" (*Entfremdung*), thus not implying that estrangement as such causes specific feelings. As is shown below, labor power must be sold, which is a type of coercion causing specific feelings.

18. See also Oiserman (1965:79).

10

Conclusions

Marx distinguishes between two concepts of human nature: general human nature, which refers to those human qualities that are invariable, and specific human nature, which consists of qualities that may vary from society to society and in history. Marx derived his concept of human nature in general from a comparison of man with animals. Estrangement results when man is prevented from living according to his human nature, that is, general human nature. Unfortunately, students of Marx have not made a clear distinction between the two concepts of human nature embodied in his work, and as a result, his theory of estrangement has frequently been misunderstood and inadequately interpreted. Our interpretation therefore stands in opposition to Petrović's (1967:146). Translating *Wesen* with "essence" instead of "nature," and using, as does Ollman, "alienation" instead of "estrangement," he says that "if alienation of man from his essence is to be possible, his essence must not be conceived as something that all men have in common." We also find Ollman's (1976:135) view to be misleading and lacking in clarity, as is evident in the following statement: "If alienation is the splintering of human nature into a number of misbegotten parts, we would expect communism to be presented as a kind of reunification." By clearly making this distinction, we have laid the foundation for a logically consistent and novel interpretation of Marx's theory of estrangement.

Marx illustrated his theory in the context of his analysis of capitalist society and with particular focus on that part of society which depends on selling labor power. Thus, it could be shown how the workers, for example, are prevented from living according to their human nature, and in which ways they can therefore be viewed as estranged. Marx's theory of estrangement does not end with the estrangement of the worker, although for various reasons he took sides with the workers and described their plight and misery in great detail. He specifically speaks also of the estrangement of the capitalist. What is it that prevents the capitalist from living according to his nature, since unlike the worker he is not forced to sell his labor power?

To resolve this problem, Marx's views on the division of labor are analyzed in detail in this book. It has been found that throughout his work[1] Marx advocates a society with a voluntary division of labor and that in his early work he directly associates estrangement with the fact that the division of labor is an involuntary one. The nature of a society's division of labor is therefore the overriding category determining whether individuals in this society are estranged.[2] This interpretation is consistent with the writings of Marx, not only with respect to his view that the capitalist is also estranged, but also with his vision of communism in which he postulates that neither estrangement nor an involuntary division of labor will exist. To regard the nature of the division of labor in a society as the decisive criterion on the basis of which man is said to be estranged must be considered a significant departure from existing interpretations of Marx's theory of estrangement.

It is maintained here that, according to Marx, the nature of the division of labor must be the central criterion deciding the existence or nonexistence of estrangement. Thus, estrangement is a dichotomous phenomenon. It exists in the absence of a voluntary division of labor, and it is not envisioned to exist under communism. Students of Marx have not tended to give central importance to the division of labor when interpreting his theory of estrangement. Rather, they generally treat the division of labor as only an aspect of estrangement, whereby it has usually been emphasized that under capital the worker must perform minute, repetitive, and unchallenging tasks. While this statement may be factually correct and Marx himself may have given

similar illustrations, such an emphasis is highly misleading when we turn to
an interpretation of Marx's theory of estrangement. As is maintained here,
the emphasis must be not on the kind of involuntary division of labor, but
on the very involuntariness of it. Marx advocates that all involuntary division
of labor be abolished. Even though an involuntary division is made more
"bearable" by humanizing work in various ways, the involuntary nature
of the division of labor persists. Similarly, to envision communism as a
society with a voluntary division of labor does not imply that individuals
will not perform different tasks. Marx's vision of the many-sided
individual is not contradicted here. There are good reasons to believe
that the individual would be many-sided under communism. However,
Marx's vision does not imply that there will be *no* "specialization" or
"routinization" of work, on a voluntary basis, under communism.
It only means that individuals are not socially coerced into performing
certain tasks. Unfortunately, this is not made as clear as it should be.
Ollman (1976:211), for example, makes the following unqualified statement: ". . . the best known descriptions of communism—a 'classless
society', a time when 'the division of labor has come to an end' and
when 'private property has been abolished'—are full alternatives."
    Ollman (1976:158-160) also fails to specify that the involuntariness
of the division of labor is manifested by the fact not only that individuals
are "locked" into one activity, but also that particularly under capital
the producers never determine what is to be produced and for what purposes.
Therefore, as long as there is commodity production, regardless of whether
individuals are "locked" into one particular activity, the division of labor
will be an involuntary one. That is, the market as such will as an impersonal
force coerce individuals into certain productive activities as long as these
individuals are dependent on commodity production for a livelihood. Here
lies the importance of Marx's insistence that production under communism
will have to be based on agreement and not exchange. For Marx, the involuntary division of labor can be abolished only by the abolition of production based on exchange, regardless of whether production on exchange
"locks" individuals into a single position.[3]
    Walter Kaufmann[4] is particularly insensitive to this important issue.
Referring to Marx's vision of a society with a voluntary division of labor
in which individuals will no longer be "locked" into an exclusive sphere
of activity, he maintains that "one of the results of the social mobility in

the United States—lateral as well as upward—is that a waiter, for example, is much less likely to feel . . . that his role defines him, freezes him. . . . Thus the alienation implicit in the division of labor is diminished significantly." Kaufmann also states that Marx's dream, to a significant degree, "is realized in the United States of America. It is not in the least unusual for the same person to have many different jobs before he is thirty."

Schacht (1971:100), on the other hand, misunderstands Marx's theory of estrangement and concept of an involuntary division of labor in another way. He faults Marx for seeing estrangement as resulting from individuals being subject to an alien will:

> Consider, for example, a camera man in a film studio, or a member of an orchestra. The "labor" of both is not and cannot be "self-directed" and "spontaneous." In each case it is directed by another man—the director or the conductor.

As a consequence, Schacht suggests that "it would seem more fruitful to drop all reference to the mediation of an 'alien will'." This conclusion is decidedly unjustified and neglects Marx's contention that

> all labour in which many individuals cooperate necessarily requires a commanding will to co-ordinate and unify the process, and functions which apply not to partial operations but to the total activity of the workshop, much as that of an orchestra conductor. This is a productive job, which must be performed in every combined mode of production (C3, p. 383; MEW, 25, p. 397).

Working under a commanding will in situations of cooperation does not automatically imply that the division of labor is an involuntary one. On the contrary, just as cooperation can be voluntary cooperation, accepting "a commanding will to co-ordinate and unify the process" can also be a voluntary act. Therefore, Marx distinguishes between this case of cooperation and coordination and that in which coordinating activity also entails coercion:

> The labour of supervision and management, arising as it does out of an antithesis, out of the supremacy of capital over labour, and being

therefore common to all modes of production based on class contradictions like the capitalist mode, is directly and inseparably connected, also under the capitalist system, with productive functions which all combined social labour assigns to individuals as their special tasks (C3, p. 386; MEW, 25, pp. 399-400; see also C3, p. 385).

ESTRANGEMENT AND THE
ABOLITION OF PRIVATE PROPERTY

When we maintain that according to Marx the division of labor must be the central criterion deciding the existence or nonexistence of estrangement, we are able to provide an answer to the long-standing debate on whether estrangement is abolished with the abolition of the private ownership of the means of production. In our view, Oiserman (1965: 84-89) is incorrect when he maintains that estrangement necessarily disappears with any socialization of the means of production. Any socialization of the means of production does not in itself guarantee a voluntary division of labor. It does not in itself guarantee a condition in which there is no domination of man by man, that is, a condition in which man is allowed to live according to his nature and is not subject to an alien will.

We need not engage in a detailed analysis of present-day socialist societies to observe that they are not the realization of Marx's vision of communism, a society in which estrangement would be nonexistent and the division of labor voluntary. Engels, we might say, foresaw the problem of present-day socialist countries when he maintained that, the more productive forces the state takes over,

the more citizens it exploits. The workers remain wage-earners, proletarians. The capitalist relationship is not abolished; it is rather pushed to an extreme. But at this extreme it changes into its opposite. State ownership of the productive forces is not the solution of the conflict, but it contains within itself the formal means, the handle to the solution (AD, pp. 312-313; MEW, 20, p. 260).[5]

A few pages later, Engels points out how communism is to be achieved (note that he refrains from using the word "state"):

The seizure of the means of production by society puts an end to commodity production, and therewith to the domination of the product over the producer. . . . Men's own social organisation which has hitherto stood in opposition to them as if arbitrarily decreed by Nature and history, will then become the voluntary act of men themselves . . . . It is humanity's leap from the realm of necessity into the realm of freedom.

To carry through this world-emancipating act is the historical mission of the modern proletariat (AD, p. 318; MEW, 20, p. 264).[6]

One may hold the opinion that this world-emancipating act of which Engels speaks has not fully occurred in present-day socialist countries, although "the handle to the solution" is there.[7]

As a consequence, it is the division of labor, and not the existence or nonexistence of private ownership of the means of production, which must serve as the criterion in deciding whether estrangement exists. According to our interpretation, then, Marx's theory of estrangement is directly extendable and applicable to socialist countries. Those who do not give central importance to the division of labor in interpreting Marx's theory of estrangement are necessarily led to other conclusions. Knecht (1975: 217), for example, asserts that Marx's theory of estrangement cannot be applied to societies in the "transitional stage" to communism. He believes that Marx's theory is only an instrument for the critique of capitalism. A critical analysis of the "transitional stage" requires first that the theory undergo a revision, and he thinks this revision is provided by Sartre. "With Sartre, the concept 'estrangement' does not only serve as an instrument in the critique of capitalism."

Ollman (1976:252-253) is compelled to maintain a similar position for similar reasons. He argues that because present-day socialist countries regulate production and consumption via a plan rather than the market, Marx's theory of estrangement "loses a full half of its meaning." He does not mean to

imply that the alienation which is found in "communist" countries cannot or should not be studied or treated theoretically, but the interaction of these men and these particular societies can only be adequately grasped by a theory which focuses on the decisive role of the plan, the

party, the state and the bureaucracy generally. Marx's theory of alienation is not such a theory.

However, Marx's theory of estrangement can very well serve as an instrument for the critique of today's socialist countries, since, according to our
interpretation, estrangement consists of the fact that man is prevented from
living according to his nature because of the existence of an involuntary
division of labor.[8] Moreover, we can do so without necessarily accepting
an existentialist position,[9] implying, as Sartre does, that estrangement is
basic to *all* human existence at all times. (See also Chapter 7 and Schaff,
1964). Marx's concept of estrangement remains a concept bound only to
definite historical periods. As Ludz (1976:8) and Remmling (1967:152)
indicate, estrangement arises with the downfall of primitive communism,
and according to Marx, it ends with communism.[10] Estrangement comes
into existence with the advent of an involuntary division of labor and is
abolished not necessarily with the abolition of private property, but with
the introduction of a voluntary division of labor. Our interpretation of
Marx's theory of estrangement is therefore also compatible with Marx's
theory of history.

A NOTE ON THE APPLICABILITY OF
MARX'S THEORY OF ESTRANGEMENT

In the preceding chapter, we show that, if Marx is not to be misinterpreted "estrangement" cannot be measured or viewed in quantitative
terms.[11] We also demonstrate that according to Marx estrangement as
such cannot meaningfully be viewed as a cause for specific behavior,
feelings, or attitudes. Since mainstream American sociology, however,
has attempted both to quantify estrangement and to postulate it as a
cause of certain behavior, feelings, or attitudes, the question arises as to
the use of Marx's theory of estrangement.

Essentially, the use of Marx's theory of estrangement is of a quite
different order than was commonly thought. Remmling (1967) already
showed how Marx is an exponent of total suspicion. Indeed, his system
of thought allows Marx to be an all-encompassing analyst and critic of
society, and his theory of estrangement is the basic building block upon
which the rest of his analysis rests. It consists of an empirical statement of

what man's nature is and a reason why, throughout much of history, man has been prevented from living according to his nature. This theory of estrangement, coupled with the demand that man be able to live according to his nature, provides Marx with both the basic framework for interpreting the social world and the goal the interpretation is to serve. Hence, the demand that all involuntary division of labor must be abolished if man is to live unestranged, that is, according to his nature. As Marx's analysis is total, his demands are total demands. Nothing short of a total change[12] can rid man of his condition of estrangement.

In attempting to measure what Marx calls estrangement and in postulating that only certain behavior, feelings, and attitudes are caused by estrangement, mainstream sociology does not consider Marx's thrust for total change.[13] However, the usefulness of Marx's theory of estrangement for sociology lies exactly in its power to critically conceptualize social reality and to employ it in the service of social change. For this to occur, however, Marx's vision of a future society based on a voluntary division of labor must not be rejected as "utopian." At least the possibility must be accepted that society could indeed be organized such as to allow for a voluntary division of labor. However, *only praxis will tell.*

NOTES

1. We disagree with Mandel (1971:161-163) who says that only with *German Ideology* did Marx view estrangement in the context of the division of labor.

2. We disagree with Plamenatz (1975:150) who maintains that Marx "does not even make it plain what kind of division of labour it is that produces alienation." Plamenatz's objections to Marx's treatment of the division of labor and its centrality to "estrangement" can be overcome by making a distinction between a voluntary and involuntary (that is, "estrangement-producing") division of labor.

3. Knecht (1975:144-145) appropriately remarks that under capital even the capitalist is subject to the independent and impersonal forces brought about by exchange, thus implying that the capitalist is also subject to an involuntary division of labor. This is in agreement with Marx's view that the capitalist is also estranged.

To argue that Marx always thought estrangement would result from the involuntary nature of the division of labor is to disagree with those (for example, Dawydow, 1964:58, 61) who maintain that only with the *German Ideology* did Marx view the voluntary division of labor as a solution to estrangement. Similarly, Tucker (1965:185) is mistaken when he claims that only with the *German Ideology* was the "alienated self-relation . . . transformed into a social relation of production, and this was given the name 'division of labour'. "

4. See Schacht (1971:xliii, xl-xliv).

5. We do not mean to say that Engels' views accurately describe the present political and economic system of present-day socialist countries. Rather, we mean that Engels touches upon the main issue involved. Thus, the issue is not whether the Soviet Union is capitalistic, but whether the means of production in that country have been "socialized" in such a way as to maintain an involuntary division of labor, that is, inequality and class relationships. For further discussions, see Bettelheim, 1976; Chavance, 1977; Sweezy, 1977a, 1977b; and Szymanski, 1977.

6. By quoting Engels here, it is unlikely that Marx's theory of estrangement will be misinterpreted, since Marx supported and cooperated with Engels in writing *Anti-Dühring* and is himself the author of a chapter. (See also Engels' preface for the edition of 1885; MEW, 20, p. 9.)

In his *Critique of the Gotha Program*, Marx also points to the necessity of abolishing class differences:

> Instead of the indefinite concluding phrase of the paragraph—"the removal of all social and political equality"—it ought to have been said that with the abolition of class differences all the social and political inequality arising from them would disappear of itself (CGP, pp. 15-16; MEW, 19, p. 26).

Abolishing inequality is not Marx's only goal. For example, in the *Manuscripts* he makes a distinction between crude communism and "true" communism. Crude communism stands for that phase in which private property has become abolished, but in which society has not eliminated coercion and the bare leveling of everyone's position:

> *Communism* is the *positive* expression of annulled private property—at first as *universal* private property. . . . This type of communism—since it negates the *personality* of man in every sphere—is but the logical expression of private property, which is this negation. General *envy* constituting itself as a power is the disguise in which greed re-establishes itself and satisfies itself, only in another way. . . . Crude communism is only the culmination of this envy and of this levelling-down proceeding from the *preconceived* minimum. It has a *definite, limited* standard. How little this annulment of private property is really an appropriation is in fact proved by the abstract negation of the entire world of culture and civilisation, the regression to the *unnatural* simplicity of the *poor* and crude man who has few needs and who has not only failed to go beyond private property, but has not yet even reached it" (CW, 3, pp. 294-295; MEW, EB 1.T., pp. 534-535).

The first positive annulment of private property—*crude* communism—is thus merely a *manifestation* of the vileness of private property, which wants to set itself up as the *positive community system* (CW, 3, p. 296; MEW, EB 1.T., pp. 535-536).

In addition to Engels' passage, we have also been able to demonstrate that Marx himself in his own writings was not endorsing just the abolition of the private ownership of the means of production. We thus have been able to strengthen our argument that the division of labor is the central criterion deciding whether or not estrangement exists.

7. In retrospect, it may be maintained that Marx and Engels were overly optimistic with respect to the ease with which class society could be abolished after the abolition of private property. This optimism is not, however, to be taken as evidence for the thesis that, for Marx and Engels, estrangement necessarily is abolished with the abolition of the private ownership of the means of production.

8. We do not endorse Ollman's view that Marx's theory of estrangement maintains its full meaning and analytical power only in the context of capitalism, a society dominated by market relationships. Rather, we reiterate that a distinction must be made between estrangement as such and the consequences of such estrangement. Because man is estranged, his life begins to be determined by forces he does not fully control. These forces at first appear in the form of personal domination and later in impersonal form, as exchange becomes universal. Regardless of the nature of the consequences, man remains estranged for Marx as long as an involuntary division of labor exists. It is our view that Marx only illustrated his theory of estrangement when analyzing capitalist society. Even by giving examples as to how man is prevented from living according to his nature under capital, his theory of estrangement does not become a theory bound to capitalism. Marx could have illustrated his theory just as well by choosing examples from feudalism, but this would have defeated his political intentions. Of course, new conceptualizations are needed for the study of the consequences of estrangement in "communist" countries and of the processes that continually prevent man from living according to his nature. But Marx's theory of estrangement need not be "adapted" since an involuntary division of labor remains an involuntary division of labor, *although the coercion manifests itself in various forms and complexities.*

9. Or to argue from an ethical point of view as Ollman seems to think.

10. It is inappropriate to speak of estrangement from nature under primitive communism—as does Krader (1975:237-238, 271-272). Although Marx does view primitive man as dominated by nature, his theory of estrangement refers only to social forms of domination. However, Marx holds that the division of labor under primitive communism was voluntary; hence, the absence of estrangement. To our knowledge, Marx also does not mention estrangement when referring to societies under primitive communism, although he views primitive communism as by no means ideal.

11. Only the consequences of estrangement can be viewed in quantitative terms. Thus, the fact that man does not fully control his life-situation—the fact that he is estranged—may result in more wealth for some and more misery for others; a feeling of strength in the bourgeoisie and a feeling of debasement in the proletariat. In contrast, estrangement as such remains a constant for all who are subject to an in-

voluntary division of labor, as much as nonestrangement is the condition for man under communism where Marx envisioned a voluntary division of labor to exist.

12. An event that has been "prepared" by the course of previous history, throughout which the consequences of estrangement are seen to have developed in such a way as to make communism realizable.

13. If "estrangement" is to be used in this way, it would be advisable either to drop the term altogether or to distinguish it clearly from Marx's use of the term.

Selected Bibliography

BOOKS

Adler, G. J. 1864. *Dictionary of the German and English Languages*. New York: Appleton.

Andrews, E. A. 1854. *Copious and Critical Latin-English Lexicon*. New York: Harper & Brothers.

Apthekar, Herbert (ed.). 1965. *Marxism and Alienation: A Symposium*. New York: Humanities Press.

Aron, Raymond. 1969. *Marxism and the Existentialists*. New York: Harper & Row.

Avineri, Shlomo. 1968. *The Social and Political Thought of Karl Marx*. Cambridge: Cambridge University Press.

Axelos, Kostas (ed.). 1976. *Alienation, Praxis and Techne in the Thought of Karl Marx*. Austin, Tex.: University of Texas Press.

Baczko, Bronislaw. 1969. *Weltanschauung, Metaphysik, Entfremdung: Philosophische Versuche*. Frankfurt: Suhrkamp.

Bedeschi, Giuseppe. 1968. *Alienazione e feticismo nel pensiero di Marx*. Bari: Laterza.

Bell, Daniel. 1967. *The End of Ideology: On the Exhaustion of Political Ideas in the Fifties*. New York: Free Press.

Berthoud, Arnand. 1974. *Travail Productif et Productivité du Travail Chez Marx*. Paris: François Maspero.

Bettelheim, Charles. 1976. *Class Struggles in the USSR. First Period: 1917-1923*. New York: Monthly Review Press.

Betteridge, H. T. (ed.). 1975. *Cassell's German and English Dictionary*. London: Cassell.

Bigo, Pierre. 1961. *Marxisme et Humanism: Introduction a l'oeuvre économique de Karl Marx*. Paris: Presses Universitaires de France.

Bloch, Ernst. 1971. *On Karl Marx*. New York: Herder.

Bottomore, Tom. 1975. *Marxist Sociology*. London: Macmillan & Co.

—— (ed.). 1973. *Karl Marx*. Englewood Cliffs, N.J.: Prentice-Hall.

Brenner, Michael, and Hermann Strasser (eds.). 1977. *Die Gesellschaftliche Konstruktion der Entfremdung*. Frankfurt: Campus.

Bryce-Laporte, Roy S., and C. S. Thomas. 1976. *Alienation in Contemporary Society: A Multidisciplinary Examination*. New York: Praeger.

Caire, G. 1956. *L'aliénation dans les oeuvres de jeunesse de Karl Marx*. Aix-en-Provence: La Pensée Universitaire.

Chiodi, P. 1976. *Sartre and Marxism*. Atlantic Highlands, N.J.: Humanities Press.

Colletti, Lucio. 1973. *Marxism and Hegel*. London: New Left Books.

——. 1972. *From Rousseau to Lenin: Studies in Ideology and Society*. New York: Monthly Review Press.

Cutler, Anthony. 1977. *Marx's Capital and Capitalism Today*. London: Routledge and Kegan Paul.

Dawydow, J.N. 1964. *Freiheit and Entfremdung*. Berlin: VEB Deutscher Verlag der Wissenschaften.

DeGeorge, Richard T. 1968. *The New Marxism: Soviet and East European Marxism Since 1956*. New York: Pegasus.

Desan, Wilfrid. 1965. *The Marxism of Jean-Paul Sartre*. Garden City, N.Y.: Doubleday.

Draper, Hal. 1977. *Karl Marx's Theory of Revolution*. New York: Monthly Review Press.

Engels, Frederick. 1942. *The Origin of the Family, Private Property and the State: In the Light of the Researches of Lewis H. Morgan*. New York: International Publishers.

——. 1935. *Herr Eugen Dühring's Revolution in Science (Anti-Dühring)*. New York: International Publishers.

Euchner, Walter, and Alfred Schmidt. 1968. *Kritik der politischen Ökonomie heute: 100 Jahre "Kapital."* Vienna: Europa Verlag.

Evans, Michael. 1975. *Karl Marx.* Bloomington, Ind.: Indiana University Press.

Fetscher, Iring. 1957. *Von Marx zur Sowjetideologie.* Frankfurt: Moritz Diesterweg.

Fischer, A. (ed.). 1970. *Die Entfremdung des Menschen in einer heilen Gesellschaft. Materialien zur Adaption und Denunziation eines Begriffs.* Munich: Jurenta (Politisches Verhalten, 2).

Fischer, Ernst (ed.). 1970. *The Essential Marx.* New York: Herder & Herder.

Freund, Wilhelm. 1844. *Gesamtwörterbuch der lateinischen Sprache.* Breslan: Georg Philipp Aderholz.

Friedrich, Manfred. 1960. *Philosophie und Ökonomie beim jungen Marx.* Berlin: Akademie-Verlag.

Fromm, Erich. 1968. *The Sane Society.* New York: Fawcett World Library.

—— (ed.). 1966. *Socialist Humanism: An International Symposium.* Garden City, N.Y.: Doubleday & Co.

——. 1961. *Marx's Concept of Man.* New York: F. Ungar Publishing Co.

Gabel, Joseph. 1975. *False Consciousness: An Essay on Reification.* New York: Harper & Row.

——. 1970. *Sociologie de l'aliénation.* Paris: Presses Universitaires.

——. 1967. *Ideologie und Schizophrenie: Formen der Entfremdung.* Frankfurt a.M.: Fischer.

Gabel, Joseph, Bernard Rousset, and Trinh Van Thao. 1974. *L'aliénation aujourd'hui.* Paris: Editions Anthropos.

Geyer, Felix R., and David R. Schweitzer (eds.). 1976. *Theories of Alienation.* Leiden: Martinus Nijhoff.

Giddens, Anthony. 1971. *Capitalism and Modern Social Theory: An Analysis of the Writings of Marx, Durkheim and Max Weber.* Cambridge: Cambridge University Press.

Godelier, Maurice. 1977. *Perspectives in Marxist Anthropology.* Cambridge: Cambridge University Press.

Guhr, Günter. 1969. *Karl Marx und theoretische Probleme der Ethnographie.* Berlin: Akademie-Verlag.

Gustafsson, Bo. 1972. *Marxismus und Revisionismus: Eduard Bernsteins Kritik des Marxismus und ihre ideengeschichtlichen Voraussetzungen.* Teil I. Frankfurt: Europäische Verlagsanstalt.

Hartmann, Klaus. 1970. *Die Marxsche Theorie: Eine Philosophische Unter-suchung zu den Hauptschriften.* Berlin: Walter De Gruyter & Co.

———. 1968. *Marxens "Kapital" in transzendental-philosophischer Sicht.* Bonn: H. Bouvier.

Heller, Agnes. 1976. *The Theory of Need in Marx.* New York: St. Martin's Press.

Hindess, Barry, and Paul Q. Hirst. 1975. *Pre-Capitalist Modes of Production.* London: Routledge & Kegan Paul.

Hodges, Donald Clark. 1974. *Socialist Humanism: The Outcome of Classical European Morality.* St. Louis: Warren H. Green.

Hoeven, Johan van der. 1976. *Karl Marx: The Roots of His Thought.* Amsterdam: Van Gorcum.

Hook, Sidney. 1936. *From Hegel to Marx: Studies in the Intellectual Development of Karl Marx.* New York: Reynal & Hitchcock.

Hunt, Richard N. 1974. *The Political Ideas of Marx and Engels: Marxism and Totalitarian Democracy, 1818-1850.* Pittsburgh: University of Pittsburgh Press.

Hyppolite, Jean. 1969. *Studies on Marx and Hegel.* Translated with an introduction, notes, and bibliography, by John O'Neill. New York: Harper & Row.

Israel, Jaochim. 1971. *Alienation: From Marx to Modern Sociology.* Boston: Allyn & Bacon.

Johnson, Frank. 1973. *Alienation: Concept, Term, Meanings.* New York: Seminar Press.

Jordan, Z. A. (ed.). 1971. *Karl Marx: Economy, Class and Social Revolution.* New York: Charles Scribner's Sons.

Joshi, P. C. 1969. *Homage to Karl Marx: A Symposium.* Delhi: People's Publishing House.

Kägi, Paul. 1965. *Genesis des historischen Materialismus.* Vienna: Europa Verlag.

Kamenka, Eugene. 1969. *Marxism and Ethics.* London: Macmillan & Co.

———. 1962. *The Ethical Foundations of Marxism.* New York: Praeger.

Kaplan, Morton A. 1976. *Alienation and Identification.* New York: The Free Press.

Klappenbach, R., and W. Steinitz. 1971. *Wörterbuch der deutschen Gegenwartssprache.* Berlin: Akademie-Verlag.

Knecht, Ingbert. 1975. *Theorie der Entfremdung bei Sartre und Marx.* Meisenheim am Glan: Verlag Anton Jain.

Kolakowski, Leszek. 1969. *Marxism and Beyond*. London: Pall Mall Press.

Koren, Henry J. 1973. *Marx and the Authentic Man: A First Introduction to the Philosophy of Karl Marx*. New York: Humanities Press.

Krader, Lawrence. 1975. *The Asiatic Mode of Production: Sources, Development and Critique in the Writings of Karl Marx*. Assen: Van Gorcum & Co.

—— (ed.). 1974. *The Ethnological Notebooks of Karl Marx*. Assen: Van Gorcum & Co.

Kühne, Karl. 1972. *Ökonomie and Marxismus, Vol. I & II*. Neuwied: Luchterhand.

Künzli, Arnold. 1966. *Karl Marx: Eine Psychographie*. Vienna: Europa Verlag.

Lefebvre, Henri. 1964. *Marx: Sa vie, son oeuvre-avec un exposé de sa philosophie*. Paris: Presses Universitaires de France.

Leković, Dragutin. 1964. *La Théorie marxiste de l'aliénation*. Belgrade: Institut Za Izucavanje Radnickog Pokreta.

Lewis, John. 1972. *The Marxism of Marx*. London: Lawrence & Wishart.

Löwenstein, Julius I. 1970. *Vision and Wirklichkeit: Marx contra Marxismus*. Basel: Kyklos-Verlag.

Lukács, Georg. 1970. *Geschichte und Klassenbewusstsein*. Neuwied: Luchterhand.

Maguire, John. 1973. *Marx's Paris Writings: An Analysis*. New York: Harper & Row.

Mandel, Ernest. 1971. *The Formation of the Economic Thought of Karl Marx*. New York: Monthly Review Press.

Mandel, Ernest, and George Novack. 1973. *The Marxist Theory of Alienation*. New York: Pathfinder Press.

Marcuse, Herbert. 1972. *Studies in Critical Philosophy*. Boston: Beacon Press.

——. 1970. *Reason and Revolution*. Boston: Beacon Press.

——. 1964. *One Dimensional Man*. Boston: Beacon Press.

Marković, Mihailo. 1974. *From Affluence to Praxis: Philosophy and Social Criticism*. Ann Arbor: University of Michigan Press.

Marx, Karl. 1975. *Wages, Price and Profit*. Peking: Foreign Languages Press.

——. 1974. *The Ethnological Notebooks*. Transcribed and edited with an Introduction by Lawrence Krader. Assen: Van Gorcum & Co.

———. 1974. *Grundrisse: Foundations of the Critique of Political Economy.* Translated with a Foreword by Martin Nicolaus. New York: Random House.

———. 1971. *Economy, Class and Social Revolution.* Edited with an introductory essay by Z. A. Jordan. New York: Charles Scribner's Sons.

———. 1970. *A Contribution to the Critique of Political Economy*, edited by Maurice Dobb. Moscow: Progress Publishers.

———. 1969. *Le Capital: Livre I.* Paris: Garnier-Flammarion.

———. 1969. *Theories of Surplus-Value*, Vol. I-III. Moscow: Progress Publishers.

———. 1964. *Pre-Capitalist Economic Formations.* Edited and with an Introduction by E. J. Hobsbawm. London: Lawrence & Wishart.

———. 1959. *Capital*, Vol. I-III. Moscow: Progress Publishers.

———. 1954. *Briefe über "Das Kapital."* Berlin: Dietz Verlag.

———. 1938. *Critique of the Gotha Programme.* New York: International Publishers.

Marx, Karl, and Friedrich Engels. n.d. *Werke.* Berlin: Dietz Verlag.

———. n.d. *Collected Works*, Vol. 1-7. New York: International Publishers.

McBridge. W. 1977. *The Philosophy of Marx.* New York: St. Martin's Press.

McLellan, David. 1975. *Karl Marx: His Life and Thought.* New York: Harper & Row.

———. 1971a. *Karl Marx: Early Texts.* Oxford: Basil Blackwell.

———. 1971b. *The Thought of Karl Marx: An Introduction.* New York: Harper & Row.

———. 1970. *Marx Before Marxism.* New York: Harper & Row.

———. 1969. *The Young Hegelians and Karl Marx.* New York: Praeger.

Meek, Ronald L. 1971. *Marx and Engels on the Population Bomb.* Berkeley, Calif.: Ramparts.

Mehring, Franz. 1964. *Karl Marx: Geschichte seines Lebens.* Berlin: Dietz Verlag.

Melotti, U. 1977. *Marx and the Third World.* Atlantic Highlands, N.J.: Humanities Press.

Mészáros, Istvan. 1972. *Marx's Theory of Alienation.* New York: Harper Torchbook.

Meyer, Alfred G. 1970. *Marxism: The Unity of Theory and Practice.* Cambridge, Mass.: Harvard University Press.

Mizruchi, Ephraim H. 1964. *Success and Opportunity.* New York: Free Press.

Oiserman, T. I. 1965. *Entfremdung als historische Kategorie*. Berlin: Dietz Verlag.

Ollman, Bertell, 1976. *Alienation: Marx's Concept of Man in Capitalist Society*. Cambridge: Cambridge University Press.

Oppolzer, Alfred, 1974. *Entfremdung und Industriearbeit: Die Kategorie der Entfremdung bei Karl Marx*. Cologne: Pahl-Rugenstein-Verlag.

Pappenheim, Fritz. 1968. *Alienation of Modern Man*. New York: Monthly Review Press.

Paul, Hermann. 1966. *Deutsches Wörterbuch*. Tübingen: Max Niemeyer.

Perroux, François. 1970. *Aliénation et société industrielle*. Paris: Éditions Gallimard.

Petrović, Gajo. 1967. *Marx in the Mid-Twentieth Century*. Garden City, N.Y.: Doubleday.

Plamenatz, John. 1975. *Karl Marx's Philosophy of Man*. New York: Oxford University Press.

Political Studies Association of the U.K. 1976. *Marx and Marx Studies*, Political Studies 24, no. 1 (March). Oxford: Clarendon Press.

Popitz, Heinrich. 1953. *Der entfremdete Mensch; Zeitkritik und Geschichtsphilosophie des jungen Marx*. Basel: Verlag für Recht und Gesellschaft.

Remmling, Gunter W. 1975. *The Sociology of Karl Mannheim*. London: Routledge & Kegan Paul.

—— (ed.). 1973. *Towards the Sociology of Knowledge: Origin and Development of a Sociological Thought Style*. London: Routledge & Kegan Paul.

——. 1967. *Road to Suspicion: A Study of Modern Mentality and the Sociology of Knowledge*. New York: Appleton-Century-Crofts.

Roberts, Paul Craig. 1971. *Alienation and the Soviet Economy: Toward a General Theory of Marxian Alienation, Organizational Principles, and The Soviet Economy*. Albuquerque: University of New Mexico Press.

Roberts, Paul Craig and M. A. Stephenson. 1973. *Marx's Theory of Exchange, Alienation and Crisis*. Stanford, Calif.: Hoover Institution Press.

Rotenstreich, Nathan. 1965. *Basic Problems of Marx's Philosophy*. Indianapolis, Ind.: Bobbs-Merrill.

Rubel, Maximilien, and Margaret Manale. 1975. *Marx Without Myth: A Chronological Study of his Life and Work*. New York: Harper and Row.

Sartre, Jean-Paul. 1976. *Critique of Dialectical Reason I: Theory of Practical Ensembles*. London: New Left Books.

Schacht, Richard. 1971. *Alienation*. Garden City, N.Y.: Doubleday.

Schaff, Adam. 1970a. *Marxism and the Human Individual*. Introduction by Erich Fromm. New York: McGraw-Hill.

——. 1970b. *Geschichte und Wahrheit*. Vienna: Europa Verlag.

——. 1964. *Marx oder Sartre*. Vienna: Europa Verlag.

——. 1954. *Zu einigen Fragen der Marxistischen Theorie der Warheit*. Berlin: Dietz Verlag.

Schmidt, Alfred. 1974. *Der Begriff der Natur in der Lehre von Marx*. Frankfurt: Europäische Verlagsanstalt.

Schwarz, Theodor. 1967. *Jean-Paul Sartre's "Kritik der dialektischen Vernunft."* Berlin: VEB Deutscher Verlag der Wissenschaften.

Selsam, Howard, and H. Martel (eds.). 1963. *Reader in Marxist Philosophy*. New York: International Publishers.

Shaw, William H. 1978. *Marx's Theory of History*. Stanford, Calif.: Stanford University Press.

Shepard, Jon M. 1971. *Automation and Alienation: A Study of Office and Factory Workers*. Cambridge, Mass.: MIT Press.

Šik, Ota. 1972. *Der dritte Weg: Die marxistisch-leninistische Theorie und die moderne Industriegesellschaft*. Hamburg: Hoffmann und Campe.

Sohn-Rethel, Alfred. 1970. *Geistige und körperliche Arbeit: Zur Theorie der gesellschaftlichen Synthesis*. Frankfurt: Suhrkamp.

Somerville, John, and H. L. Parsons (eds.). 1974. *Dialogues on the Philosophy of Marxism*. Westport, Conn.: Greenwood Press.

Suhrkamp (ed.). 1967. *Folgen einer Theorie: Essays über "Das Kapital" von Karl Marx*. Frankfurt: Suhrkamp.

Swingewood, Alan. 1975. *Marx and Modern Social Theory*. New York: John Wiley & Sons.

Terray, Emmanuel. 1972. *Marxism and "Primitive" Societies*. New York: Monthly Review Press.

Thier, Erich. 1957. *Das Menschenbild des jungen Marx*. Göttingen: Vanderhoeck & Ruprecht.

Torrance, John. 1977. *Estrangement, Alienation and Exploitation*. New York: Columbia University Press.

Tucker, Robert C. (ed.). 1972. *The Marx-Engels Reader*. New York: W. W. Norton & Co.

——. 1969. *The Marxian Revolutionary Idea*. New York: W. W. Norton & Co.

——. 1965. *Philosophy and Myth in Karl Marx*. Cambridge: Cambridge University Press.

Venable, Vernon. 1966. *Human Nature: The Marxian View.* New York: Meridian Books.

Walton, P., and A. Gamble. 1972. *From Alienation to Surplus Value.* London: Sheed & Ward.

Wartburg, Walther. 1952. *Französisches Etymologisches Wörterbuch.* Basel: Helbing & Lichtenhahn.

Wyss, Dieter. 1969. *Marx und Freud: Ihr Verhältnis zur modernen Anthropologie.*

Zeitlin, Irving M. 1967. *Marxism: A Re-Examination.* Cincinnati: Van Nostrand Reinhold.

Zitta, Victor. 1964. *George Lukács' Marxism, Alienation, Dialectics, Revolution: A Study in Utopia and Ideology.* The Hague: Martinus Nijhoff.

ARTICLES

Archibald, W. Peter. 1976. "Using Marx's Theory of Alienation Empirically." In R. Felix Geyer and D. R. Schweitzer (eds.), *Theories of Alienation.* Leiden: Martinus Nijhoff, pp. 59-77.

Avineri, Shlomo. 1973. "Marx's Vision of Future Society," *Dissent* 20, no. 3 (Summer): 323-332.

Barakat, Halim. 1969. "Alienation: A Process of Encounter Between Utopia and Reality," *British Journal of Sociology* 20, no. 1 (March): 1-11.

Bell, Daniel. 1977. "Review Essay: The One and Future Marx," *American Journal of Sociology* 83, no. 1 (July): 187-197.

——. 1959. "The 'Rediscovery' of Alienation: Some Notes Along the Quest for the Historical Marx," *Journal of Philosophy* 56, no. 24 (November): 933-952.

Braybrooke, David. 1958. "Diagnosis and Remedy in Marx's Doctrine of Alienation," *Social Research* 25, no. 3 (Autumn): 325-345.

Buhr, Manfred. 1966. "Entfremdung—Philosophische Anthropologie— Marxkritik," *Deutsche Zeitschrift für Philosophie* 14, no. 7: 806-834.

Chavance, Bernard. 1977. "On the Relations of Production in the USSR," *Monthly Review* 29, no. 1 (May): 1-13.

Dean, D. 1961. "Alienation, Its Meaning and Measurement," *American Sociological Review* 26, no. 5 (October): 753-758.

Easton. Loyd D. 1970. "Alienation and Empiricism in Marx's Thought," *Social Reserach* 37, no. 3 (Autumn): 402-428.

Fetscher, Iring. 1973. "Karl Marx on Human Nature," *Social Research* 40, no. 3 (Autumn): 443-468.

Feuer, Lewis. 1963. "What Is Alienation? The Career of a Concept." In M. Stein and A. Vidich (eds.), *Sociology on Trial*. Englewood Cliffs, N.J.: Prentice-Hall.

Fischer, Claude S. 1976. "Alienation: Trying to Bridge the Chasm," *British Journal of Sociology* 27, no. 1 (March): 35-49.

Fischer, S. 1973. "On Urban Alienations and Anomie: Powerlessness and Social Isolation," *American Sociological Review* 38, no. 3 (June): 311-326.

Heise, W. 1965. "Ueber die Entfremdung und ihre Ueberwindung," *Deutsche Zeitschrift für Philosophie* 13:684-719.

Horton, John. 1964. "The Dehumanization of Anomie and Alienation: A Problem in the Ideology of Sociology," *British Journal of Sociology* 15, no. 4 (December): 283-300.

Hunt, E. K. 1978. "A Comment on William LeoGrande's Approach to the 'Young Marx'," *Science & Society* 42. no. 1 (Spring): 84-90.

Israel, Joachim. 1976. "Alienation and Reification." In R. Felix Geyer and D. R. Schweitzer (eds.), *Theories of Alienation*. Leiden: Martinus Nijhoff, pp. 59-77.

———. 1974. "Alienation and Reification," Paper presented at the 8th World Congress of Sociology in Toronto, Canada.

Jahn, W. 1957. "Der ökonomische Inhalt des Begriffes der Entfremdung der Arbeit in den Frühschriften von K. Marx," *Wirtschaftswissenschaft* 6:848-865.

Kirsch, Barbara A., and J. J. Lengermann. 1972. "An Empirical Test of Robert Blauner's Ideas on Alienation in Work as Applied to Different Types of Jobs in a White-Collar Setting," *Sociology and Social Research* 56, no. 2 (January): 180-195.

Krader, Lawrence. 1976. "Social Evolution and Social Revolution," *Dialectical Anthropology* 1 (February): 109-120.

———. 1975a. "Marxist Anthropology: Principles and Contradictions, Part I: Society, Individual and Person," *International Review of Social History* 20:236-272.

———. 1975b. "Marxist Anthropology: Principles and Contradiction, Part II: Relations to Nature; Abstract and Concrete Labor," *International Review of Social History* 20:424-449.

———. 1973. "The Works of Marx and Engels in Ethnology Compared," *International Review of Social History* 18:223-75.

Lamb, Helen E., and S. Lehrman. 1961. "On Alienation: Two Contrasting Views," *Science & Society* 25, no. 2 (Summer): 260-269.

Lee, Alfred McClung. 1972. "An Obituary for 'Alienation'," *Social Problems* 20, no. 1 (Summer): 121-127.

LeoGrande, William. 1977. "An Investigation into the 'Young Marx' Controversy," *Science & Society* 41, no. 2 (Summer): 129-151.

Lewis, John. 1964. "Marx's View of Alienation," *Marxism Today* 8:17-22.

Lindsay, Jack. 1964. "Alienation Under Socialism," *Marxism Today* 8 (November): 353-356.

Ludz, Peter C. 1976. "Alienation as a Concept in the Social Sciences." In Felix R. Geyer and D. R. Schweitzer (eds.), *Theories of Alienation.* Leiden: Martinus Nijhoff, pp. 3-37.

Marx, Karl. 1972. "Marginal Notes on Adolph Wagner's Lehrbuch der politischen Ökonomie." *Theoretical Practice* 5 (Spring): 40-65.

McLellan, David. 1969. "Marx's View of the Unalienated Society," *Review of Politics* 31, no. 4 (October): 459-466.

Meja, Volker. 1975. Review Article of *Knowledge and Social Structure: An Introduction to the Classical Argument in the Sociology of Knowledge,* by Peter Hamilton. In *Contemporary Sociology* 4, no. 2 (March): 101-103.

Merland, P. 1970. "Alienation in Marx's Political Economy and Philosophy." In Maurice Natanson (ed.), *Phenomenology and Social Reality.* The Hague: Martinus Nijhoff, pp. 195-212.

Meyer, Heinz. 1975. "Der Sport als Medium der Selbstverwirklichung und Entfremdung," *Zeitschrift für Soziologie* 4, no. 1 (January): 70-81.

Middleton, R. 1963. "Alienation, Race, and Education," *American Sociological Review* 28, no. 6 (December): 973-977.

Nagvi, S. 1973. "Marx on Pre-British Indian Society and Economy," *Socialist Digest* 7 (March): 36-71.

Nasser, A. 1975. "Marx's Ethical Anthropology," *Philosophy and Phenomenological Research* 35, no. 4 (June): 484-500.

Neal, A. G., and S. Rettig. 1967. "On the Multidimensionality of Alienation," *American Sociological Review* 32, no. 1 (February): 54-67.

Nettler, G. 1957. "A Measure of Alienation," *American Sociological Review* 22, no. 6 (December): 670-677.

Oiserman, T. I. 1962. "Le problème de l'aliénation dans les travaux de jeunesse de Marx," *Recherches internationales à la lumière du marxisme,* no. 33-34: 63-82.

——. 1962. "Das Problem der Entfremdung im Zerrspiegel der bürgerlichen und revisionistischen 'Kritik' des Marxismus," *Deutsche Zeitschrift für Philosophie* 10:1147-1161.

Ollman, Bertell. 1967-1968. "Marx's Use of 'Class'," *American Journal of Sociology* 73, no. 5 (March): 573-580.

O'Neill, John. 1964. "The Concept of Estrangement in the Early and Later Writings of Karl Marx," *Philosophy and Phenomenological Research* no. 25, 1 (September): 64-84.

Overend, Tronn. 1975. "Alienation: A Conceptual Analysis," *Philosophy and Phenomenological Research* 35, no. 3 (March): 301-322.

Pearlin, L. I. 1962. "Alienation from Work: A Study of Nursing Personnel," *American Sociological Review* 27, no. 3 (June): 314-326.

Piccone, Paul. 1975. "Reading the *Grundrisse:* Beyond 'Orthodox' Marxism," *Theory & Society* 2, no. 2 (Summer): 235-257.

——. 1972. "Utopia and the Concrete Overcoming of Alienation," *Praxis* 8, no. 1:93-102.

Rosen, Z. 1970. "The Influence of Bruno Bauer on Marx' Concept of Alienation," *Social Theory and Practice* 1, no. 2 (Fall): 50-69.

Rousset, Bernard. 1974. "Conclusions." In Joseph Gabel, B. Rousset, and Trinh Van Thao (eds.), *L'aliénation aujourd'hui.* Paris: Éditions anthropos, pp. 250-257.

Rovatti, Pier Aldo. 1973. "The Critique of Fetishism in Marx's Grundrisse," *Telos,* No. 17 (Fall): 56-70.

Seeman, Melvin. 1976. "Empirical Alienation Studies: An Overview." In R. F. Geyer, and D. R. Schweitzer (eds.), *Theories of Alienation.* Leiden: Martinus Nijhoff, pp. 265-305.

——. 1972a. "The Signals of '68: Alienation in Pre-Crisis France," *American Sociological Review* 37, no. 4 (August): 385-402.

——. 1972b. "Alienation and Knowledge-Seeking: A Note on Attitude and Action," *Social Problems* 20, no. 1 (Summer): 3-17.

——. 1971a. "The Urban Alienations: Some Dubious Theses from Marx to Marcuse," *Journal of Personality and Social Psychology* 19, no. 2 (August): 135-143.

——. 1971b. "Alienation: A Map," *Psychology Today* (August): 83-84, 94-95.

——. 1971c. "Community and Control in a Metropolitan Setting." In P. Orleans and W. R. Ellis, Jr. (eds.), *Race, Change and Urban Society.* Beverly Hills, Calif.: Sage Publications, pp. 423-450.

——. 1967. "On the Personal Consequence of Alienation in Work," *American Sociological Review* 32, no. 1 (February): 273-285.

——. 1959. "On the Meaning of Alienation," *American Sociological Review* 24, no. 5 (October): 783-791.

Shepard, Jon M., and T. R. Panko. 1974. "Alienation and Social Referents," *Sociology and Social Research* 59, no. 1 (October): 55-61.

Soubise, L. 1967. "L'aliénation politique chez les néo-marxistes," *Projet* (April): 389-408.

Strmiska, Zdenek. 1974. "Structure de la problématique, sociologique marxienne et notion d'aliénation." In Joseph Gabel, B. Rousset, and Trinh Van Thao (eds.), *L'aliénation aujourd'hui.* Paris: Éditions anthropos, pp. 43-117.

Sullivan, J. P. (ed.). 1975. "Marxism and the Classics," *Arethusa* 8, no. 1 (Spring): 5-201.

Sweezy, Paul M. 1977a. "Bettelheim on Revolution from Above: The USSR in the 1920s," *Monthly Review* 29, no. 5 (October): 1-20.

——. 1977b. "On the Relations of Production in the USSR" (Reply to Bernard Chavance), *Monthly Review* 29 no. 1 (May): 13-20.

Szymansky, Al. 1977. "Socialism or Capitalism in the USSR," *Science and Society* 41, no. 3 (Fall): 338-344.

Tatsis, N., and G. Zito. 1975. "Marx, Durkheim and Alienation: Toward a Heuristic Typology," *Social Theory and Practice* 3, no. 2 (Fall): 223-245.

Tudor, Bill. 1972. "A Specification of Relationships Between Job Complexity and Powerlessness," *American Sociological Review* 37, no. 5 (October): 596-604.

Wallimann, Isidor. 1979. Review of "Estrangement, Alienation and Exploitation: A Sociological Approach to Historical Materialism" by John Torrance. New York: Columbia University Press, 1977. *Contemporary Sociology* 8, no. 2 (March): 270-271.

——. 1975. "Alienation: In Marx and Modern Empirical Sociology," *Zeitschrift für Soziologie* 4, no. 3 (July): 273-282.

Walton, P. A. Gamble, and J. Coulter. 1970. "Image of Man in Marx," *Social Theory and Practice*, 1, no. 2 (Fall): 69-85.

Welskopf, E. Ch. 1965. "Entfremdung historisch gesehen," *Deutsche Zeitschrift für Philosophie* 13: 711-720.

Winfield, Richard. 1976. "The Logic of Marx's Capital," *Telos,* No. 27 (Spring): 111-139.

Index

About the Author

Isidor Wallimann is a Lecturer at the School of Social Work, Basle, and at the Institute of Sociology, University of Bern, Switzerland. He has written numerous articles for scholary publications including *Sociology, The Review of Black Political Economy,* and *Zeitschrift fuer Soziologie.*